MORE RULES
OF FUNDRAISING

Douglas K. Shaw

published by

DOUGLAS SHAW
& Associates
FUNDRAISING COUNSEL
Donor-Focused Strategic Marketing®
630.562.1321 ※ www.douglasshaw.com

FIRST EDITION

PRAISE FOR
THE RULES OF FUNDRAISING

Doug Shaw is among a very small handful of the most outstanding direct response fundraisers in the country. His firm is one of the largest and most effective.

Now he has a book that exposes us to all his years of experience and expertise. It's an amazing book.

Doug claims he doesn't believe in rules. Then he gives us 35 rules that are profound and inviolate. It's like opening up a treasure chest.

This book is replete with stories of the great and near-great. You get to know what has worked and what hasn't. And you get to know a great deal about Doug and what makes him tick.

You don't have to be in direct mail to prize this volume. Doug has made a valuable contribution to the field and our profession. This book is a must. Get one for your desk, for quick reference, and for your library.

- JEROLD PANAS
Executive Partner — Jerold Panas, Linzy & Partners

INTRODUCTION

I'm not particularly fond of rules. In fact I was cautioned by a publisher to supplant the word "Rules" with something less threatening like, "Principles." As you can see from the title of this book, I decided to go with "rules." Besides, whenever I've spoken at conferences, seminars, or to a group of CEOs or board members, I have experienced great encouragement to cite the "rules" for them while they feverishly attempt to write them all down.

It's my hope that these rules will help you further along your journey in the great enterprise of philanthropy. Let me be quick to say these are not MY rules. They are industry best-practices known to those who have labored long in the fields of fundraising. I only wish someone had written them down as I was making my own way through the victories and failures of nonprofit development.

What DOES belong to me are the life stories that are intended to serve as a context or illustration for each rule. Some are from my early years and others are from the front lines of my life as a fundraising consultant. All are written to introduce or illustrate the rules themselves.

This book you're reading is a continuation of *The Rules*

of Fundraising, but you don't need to read the first volume to benefit from the second.

However, there is benefit in knowing the first four rules of fundraising prior to diving into numbers 36-70 here. In fact they are the only four rules that are prerequisite for gleaning the most from this book. Here they are in an abbreviated form:

Rule #1: *There are rules in fundraising.*

There are rules in fundraising, just like there are in quantum physics or any other field of study. Granted, these rules are not as complicated and involve a fairly low level of mathematical ability or else I'd be searching on LinkedIn for another job.

Let me be clear, following the rules won't guarantee success, but NOT following them will likely lead you to a much longer learning curve and quite possibly . . . failure.

There is no standardized governing or accrediting body specifically tasked with training or evaluating the experience and competency of individual fundraisers. The Evangelical Council for Financial Accountability (ECFA) sets, monitors, and reports on ministry efficiency, but not on the effectiveness of individuals. The legal profession has the bar exam, and medical schools have their boards, and accounting has its Generally Accepted Accounting Practices (GAAP), but philanthropy is largely a self-governed, self-evaluating community. There is the Certified Fundraising Executive (CFRE) and the Credentialed Christian Nonprofit Leader (CCNL) certifications, and they take a significant step toward measuring the body of knowledge mastered by fundraisers, but this book is about behavior rather than knowledge. It's about what works. It's about the rules that govern the successful raising of money for the cause you so dearly love.

Rule #2: *Nobody knows all the rules . . . including old guys like me.*

It's difficult to find people inside or outside the nonprofit world who have knowledge of most of the rules. Many people believe their background in marketing or business qualifies them to serve as fundraisers; a great number of them have discovered that is rarely the case.

Fundraising has its own rules, and most marketing folks find themselves struggling until they discover this ego-bruising truth. Unfortunately it's the ministry that has to suffer until the marketing professional comes to realize this.

A word to the board member or CEO of a nonprofit; marketing experience does not equal fundraising experience. Of course the reverse is true as well. Most seasoned fundraisers will tell you that there are overlaps between the disciplines of marketing and fundraising, but not enough to qualify a marketing person as a fundraiser. My most positive experiences with marketing people coming into the world of philanthropy is when the marketing professional recognizes the truth of this early on and simply says, "I'm from marketing, not fundraising. I have a lot to learn; will you teach me?"

Even after a lifetime of direct response fundraising, any honest craftsman will tell you, they don't know it all. Nobody knows ALL the rules of fundraising, but this old guy can tell you, you have to start somewhere. We all did. Admitting to

MORE RULES OF FUNDRAISING

yourself that you don't know much is truthful and believable. It's probably most important that you can admit this to yourself. This is a character-forming insight that can free you up to become curious and humble, two traits that can help you greatly as you seek knowledge from those who have traveled the trail a little longer than you. Even old guys like me have mentors, and I count them as personal gifts to the spirit.

Rule #3: *Neither you nor I get to make the rules.*

An extremely frustrating fact is that neither you nor I get to make the rules. Like gold, all we can do is be relentless in seeking to discover the rules of fundraising. It requires a lot of pickaxe work, shoveling, and back-breaking labor to amass enough rules to learn the difference between real gold and fool's gold. The veteran fundraiser will recognize the truth of this since they have done the work, carefully sifted through soil, and spotted shiny nuggets amongst the stones along the banks of The River of Opportunity. That's why I've written these books. It's kind of a starter set of rules, if you will, to get you going on your own pilgrimage.

Again, we don't get to make the rules, they just exist!

"So," you might ask, "if the rules aren't written down and few people can tell me what they are, how do I know they exist?" If the words, "Trust me" don't satisfy you, you may want to keep reading!

Knowing your limitations, where instinct and intelligence can lead you astray, is a place many well-meaning people are afraid to go. It says a lot about us, I guess. Sometimes we think we know something we really don't. Or perhaps we feel guilty because we've been hired to do something and we think we should know our craft better than we actually do. Worst case, it may feed our ego to be able to think we have the position and power to make up our own rules. As a fundraising consultant I see this kind of self-delusion much more often than I would like. For me it's one of the most heartbreaking experiences I encounter in my work.

When a board member, CEO, or Director of Development begins to espouse their personal philosophy, I know we're all in trouble. It usually begins with a statement like this: "You see, our organization is unique . . ." I fell prey to it myself when I first started out, and it didn't serve me well. It's pretty embarrassing to end a year of working long and difficult hours and have only a pouch full of glittering fool's gold as a result.

So how do you ensure that you are discovering the time-tested rules of fundraising and not just somebody's personal opinion? Let's continue down the road a bit and see where all of this leads...

Rule #4: *What you think you know about fundraising doesn't matter.*

As sad as it is, it doesn't really matter what you or I want to think we know about a fundraising approach or strategy. It hurts just to write it. In fact, much of reality hurts; getting splinters, stubbing toes, getting a root canal, growing fat, growing old and fat . . . you get the idea. I'd like to think my life experience or my bachelor's and master's degrees count for something. Alas, with all sadness, they don't. What counts in fundraising and football is the score. Did my attempt to score put points on the board, or did I get sacked?

Experienced fundraisers know the awful truth of this rule. To continue with the sports metaphor, a coach who doesn't win, doesn't keep his/her job. It's as simple as that. Your organization may like you, and I sincerely hope they do, but your board and CEO are evaluating you on your ability to provide financial resources for your cause, not on your undeniable passion for your mission (which is important) or the fact that you always bring donuts on Tuesdays (which for some of your less goal-oriented colleagues may be even more important).

Unfortunately "what we think we know about fundraising" is a cow patty many fundraisers can't resist stepping in! I can usually spot a person who's about to mess up their shoes within about 30 minutes of meeting them. One trait they all share is their need to make assumptions rather than ask questions. Assumptions can get you smeared green from the top of your head all the way down to the bottoms of your feet, or at the very least, put slimy stuff between your toes, whereas questions can lead you to the places where the open pastures are.

Questions can help you determine the length and width of the field. They can help you determine the kind of cow patties ahead of you, empower you with knowledge that can determine if they are hard and white or soft and gooey, (I'm afraid my rural upbringing is showing here), or at least lead you to a friendly farmer who can suggest an alternative path (like wading in the river). A good fundraiser knows that what they want to believe doesn't matter.

Ecclesiastes says it well, "Vanity of vanities, all is vanity"

(Ecclesiastes 1:2). If we want to follow the rules, it requires that we part with as much of our vanity as possible. I know my ego smarts at having to acknowledge that I even have an ego. But I do! And I suppose, like most of us, you do too. In order to follow the rules of effective fundraising, we would be better served to unfasten all the buttons and belts of our ego, slide out of any psychological defenses we may have, and lay them gently on the ground. Fully exposed, we have to face the fact that we are defenseless. This is where the strength and wisdom are found, in our defenselessness.

Well, these are the first four rules. Now you can dip into whatever rule appeals to you most and hopefully you'll feel empowered to sharpen your fundraising skills, dust off what you may have already known, and share these with your staff and administration for their own personal growth.

I'm so glad to share with you *The Rules,* which are one traveler's gift to another, with stories and examples to help you get to where you feel the road is calling you.

NOTES:

RULE #36
"Saying thank you to donors is necessary and profitable!"

There's a great Wallace Shawn (Vizzini) line from the classic movie, *The Princess Bride,* that always come to mind whenever I hear the annual poll results of donors' top two giving complaints: (1) not being thanked for a recent gift, and (2) they are never told what their gift has accomplished. It's actually a word, more than a line, but I can still hear the lispy word pouring out of Vizzini's mouth over and over again, "incontheivable!"

I can't, even for a moment, conceive of receiving a gift, of any amount, without saying "thank you" to the person who just made the decision to take the heart action of giving a gift to my cause. I can't fathom it! I don't understand it! To me, it's simply "incontheivable!"

But, the fact is, it's altogether true. Most organizations expend their energies trying to come up with strategies, tactics, messaging and channels that will move a person to the point of clicking GIVE NOW or pulling out their checkbook and hand writing their organization's name and the dollar amount of their gift, and then dating it and signing their own name. They put their check into an envelope, rummage through their desk or kitchen junk drawer to find a stamp, affix it to the envelope, and then they have to post it in a mailbox! That's a lot of work in today's electronic world! Here, in North America, that is still what most donors do. They write a check! And you know what they hear in return? Nothing! Nada! Zilch! It's absolutely incontheivable!

The other half of this awkward exchange, if you remember, is the donor is never told what their giving has accomplished! Now, to this old fundraiser, this is adding insult to injury. The nonprofit has injured their relationship with their donor by not saying "thank you," but there's MORE! Now they get to insult the donor, by not informing them just how their generosity has changed or saved someone's life. In essence, this kind of insensitivity is depriving generous people of the joy of giving! Now, I know ministries and organizations don't purposefully set out to do this. It seems to me they just haven't taken the time to put themselves into the place of the donor. With all the pressure we feel, as fundraisers, to raise the maximum amount of money while spending the least amount possible, it's pretty understandable how some organizations would let this opportunity to thank and inform donors what their gift has done slip past them (we'll spend much more time on this in rule #40). But, here's the part I find hard to understand...by sending the donor a well-crafted thank-you letter, receipt and a reply envelope, at least 20-30% of the receipt envelopes will come back to you with yet another gift! Now, I must admit that sometimes I exaggerate in order to make my point; not this time...I promise! Some organizations receive up to 1/3 of their total donated income from receipt or "bounce-back" income. That's a lot of money!

Here's a true story. A beloved ministry and client had decided to invest heavily in donor acquisition. They needed to grow their donor base in order to support the growth of their ministry. So every fall they would mail several million pieces of direct mail, place inserts in newspapers and special stuffers into utility bills, all seeking to move the people of their city to help feed homeless people. It worked exceptionally well! The mail and the money poured in. So much so that temporary employees were hired to assist with data entry and processing thank-you/receipt letters. But something went terribly awry...the Chief Development Officer became ill and was ordered home, by her physician, for extensive bed rest. An unsupervised employee made an uninformed decision...

In order to save time, the employee decided that he would either have to expend his energy entering gift data OR processing and mailing thank-you/receipt letters. He decided to enter gift data. No letters or receipts were sent to newly acquired donors for over six weeks! Hundreds of thousands of dollars were lost (because the 20-30% who should have received a thank you would have given again). But even worse, many of the newly acquired donors were insulted and did not contribute again. Now, this could happen to anybody who doesn't know the rules of fundraising. In this case, the employee was being continually asked, "How many days of mail are yet to be entered?" Wanting to please his employer, he put his focus on the thing he thought was most important (i.e., gift data entry). He was mortified to later learn just how much his decision cost the ministry. That's why this rule exists: "Saying 'Thank You' to donors is necessary and profitable," and...it's also the right thing to do!

NOTES:

RULE #37
"The left hand does need to know what the right hand is doing."

Have you ever climbed up the outside of a silo on a dairy farm? No, I suppose not. Very few non-farmers have. I remember my own excursion when I was six years old. We were living in Missouri, and my dad had just taken a job as a farmhand. Now, to someone of my young age climbing inside a ladder, surrounded by a cage, several stories up into the sky appeared to be one of the cooler things a kid could do...until I arrived at the top, that is. My dad had ascended just ahead of me, but when I looked up I saw his booted foot disappearing through an opening near the top of the silo.

I sped up to see the mystery at the top of farm world. But the closer I came to the door, the more my eyes began to sting and my nose encountered a very foul rotten vegetable kind of smell. Of course, as a six-year-old, all vegetables smelled rotten, but this pungent odor was more of a gas-like substance that hung in the air.

Inside the silo, I could hear my dad talking to the farmer. Every word echoed out the door above me. Now as I neared the opening my sense of mystery was waning sharply with every gaseous breath.

Peering through the man-sized hole, breathing through my

mouth, I could see a ladder attached to the inside of the silo and my dad and the farmer standing about 12 feet down on top of the source of my agony...corn silage (basically chopped up, rotting corn stalks). The heat of the methane gas rising from the silage was pushing past my face, gagging me and forcing tears to run down my cheeks. I'd seen all I could handle. The mystery was no more. It had been replaced by something I never cared to experience again.

I've never looked at a silo in the same way since.

At the time of writing, it's quite in vogue to describe contiguous but non-intersecting organizational functions as being "siloed." To put it more simply, this occurs when departments within an organization aren't communicating adequately. This is an apt description of dysfunctional behavior or communication, if you ask this old fundraiser.

Unfortunately, there really is no mystery to it. Silos develop quite easily and appear to be the natural state of humanity. I very seldom see malice causing silos to pop up, but rather a momentary neglect of vigilance. I know I helped to create my own share of silos in my day.

Perhaps I was inspired as a small boy, by this exposure to rotten cornstalks...but I have spent much of my life trying to help tear down silos. Here are just a few of the silos that are most commonly found inside ministries:

- Annual fund departments
- Direct mail departments
- Marketing departments
- Publications
- Planned giving departments

- Major gift departments
- Capital campaigns
- Digital departments
- Public relations departments

I fully realize that I may have just described your entire advancement team! But don't feel alone, there are silos wherever there are people who work together toward a common cause. I'm choosing to focus here on those most closely related to fundraising since we are, after all, looking at the rules of fundraising. In this case, the rule, again, is, "The left hand DOES need to know what the right hand is doing." Remember, it's not my rule; it's an industry rule. We just have to figure out how to follow it.

In fundraising, silos are dangerous to the health of your ministry or organization. Whenever a particular department or channel of communication stands totally on its own, apart from all others within the organization, unintentional consequences often result. Here's how it plays out in the life of a donor:

Mary Smith, a longtime friend and donor to your ministry, goes to her mailbox. It's overflowing! Of course there's the mandatory credit card solicitations, and catalogs, a magazine or two, her electric bill and three mailings from your ministry! She briefly peels through her mail stack as she walks back into her house, muttering something about "killing way too many trees." When she hits the section where your ministry's three mailings are grouped together, she tosses the other stuff on her kitchen counter and takes your stuff over to her computer. Using the back flap of an envelope, she looks for your web address and looks up at her computer screen to enter your site. Her email screen is up, and before she can type in your website, she spots an email blast from...you guessed it, your ministry. "This is absolutely ridiculous," she says in disgust.

If Mary is a proactive person, she may do you the service of emailing you a complaint. She might just decide to take out her pen and write the dreaded words, "Remove me from your list," on the reply device from one of the three mailings she's just received. But Mary is proactive; most people aren't. Most people just throw everything away that comes from you and stop giving. They also block you from their email. You've just lost a good friend and supporter!

Now, nobody wanted this to happen. In fact, the whole thing stinks (I smell a silo here)! The good news here is that what Mary experienced is completely avoidable, but it does take intentionality!

Have you seen some of the newer silos that farmers are using today? There are all kinds of pipes running from one silo to another. They're all linked so that silage or grain can be moved from one silo to another. The interconnectedness allows for a much smoother and more coordinated operation. The same can be true for organizations that are aware of the silos in their ministry. Creating intentional and helpful interdepartmental communications can be done, but it isn't easy.

If your left hand is going to know what your right hand is doing, it will require several things:
- Acknowledge that there is a problem
- Identify a specific illustration of what the problem looks like, e.g., Mary's handwriting on the reply device she

so kindly mailed back to you. I recommend a follow-up call to ask Mary why she's asked to be removed from your mailing list.

- Document your conversation with Mary
- Present your findings to the heads of the departments within your advancement area
- Present them with a solution, i.e., a comprehensive communication calendar that is agreed upon or controlled by your head of advancement
- Abide by the schedule

Once you do this, it will help to propel your organization forward, raise more money and...really clear the air!

NOTES:

RULE #38
"Madison Avenue is right! (Multichannel = market penetration)"

This rule is a bit provocative, isn't it? I can't count the number of times I've heard a CEO tell me, "Now, I know we need strategies, but I don't want any of that Madison Avenue slickness used in representing this ministry!"

So what am I doing invoking Madison Avenue? Well the simple explanation is...sometimes even Madison Avenue gets it right! In this rule, they spent billions learning things that ministries can put to good use.

Even though philanthropy didn't invent multichannel promotion, we've greatly benefitted from the concept. Madison Avenue carefully studied the positive effects of using every channel possible to promote their clients' products or services.

To the average person the phrase "Integrated Multichannel Campaign" could be quite confusing. Conversely, to anyone involved in marketing or fundraising, it not only makes sense, but it is now a part of the daily vocabulary for those on the forefront of their craft.

For the Cold War generation, we witnessed the advertising world's increased use of billboards, cab backs, newspapers, radio, television, magazines, blimps and large murals on buildings all proclaiming the arrival of IBM's Personal Computer. We saw the great mouthwash wars of Scope and Listerine, the ongoing struggle for dominance of Coke and Pepsi, and a myriad of other consumer products played out before us in and on ANYTHING that could carry a message.

For those of us born into a world of Mac versus PC, Blackberry versus iPhone, we may have accepted that integrated, multichannel campaigns were simply all part of the world in which we live. We learned to use social media at the same time that we learned to walk and talk.

Now we may find ourselves working side-by-side in ministries in need of getting out our message and funding it with donated dollars; different generations, all in the same work force, sharing the same passion for our ministry but, perhaps, with radically different ideas about how to communicate.

Regardless of our generational origins or personal context, we all live in a world that offers more communication channels than at ANY time in history. That's a pretty challenging reality if you take a moment to ponder it. Equally challenging is the responsibility of discerning the most useful ways to engage people with the message of your ministry.

ALL CHANNELS ARE NOT CREATED EQUAL

If we were to set out to use the many channels available to us, and we desired to be highly discerning, making certain that biblical stewardship principles, e.g., the Parable of the Talents in Matthew 25, guided our journey, there are many principles we would need to know. The overarching principle would need to be: We are, for a fact, using every channel available to us, in the most impactful way. Because we are driven by a desire for excellence in the name of the Master, we don't have the luxury of guessing, or assuming. We simply have to KNOW what channel should be used and for what purpose. It's my deepest desire, here, that you can experience success in building an integrated, multichannel campaign.

STEP #1:

It's my experience that in building a campaign we must rid ourselves of any form of ego, assumption, or theory. That's right. In communications and fundraising, WE are usually the single largest impediment to our own success. You will have a much greater opportunity for success if you disallow yourself both thoughts and words that may trump reality, e.g., statements like: "I think," "I want," and "I believe."

Over the years, successful campaigns have been based upon this simple yet harsh reality: "What we're looking for in a successful campaign is what works, not what I think will work!" This is where knowing the rules of fundraising has served experienced fundraisers well.

STEP #2:

Identify and document the single most important fundraising outcome of your campaign. For most ministries it will be something like: "We need to raise $500,000 to fund this unprecedented opportunity facing our ministry in order to _____."

Other, non-fundraising outcomes may involve:
- Growth of your ministry programs
- Engagement of your constituents
- Awareness of your ministry or the issues you seek to address

But harsh reality says that you can only have one fundraising outcome!

STEP #3:

Identify all of the channels available to your ministry. Reality is, not every channel in existence will be either available to you or affordable. So identify and list which channels are indeed available, e.g.:
- Face-to-face cultivation of individual major donors
- Foundation proposals
- Church interest and support
- Corporate interest and support
- Special events
- Planned giving
- Direct mail
- Email
- Mobile
- Social media
- Website
- Publicity
- Electronic media
- Print advertising (magazines, newsletters, newspapers...you get the idea)

- Outdoor advertising (billboards, cab backs, bus cards, etc.)
- Other channels unique to your ministry

STEP #4:

Developing a sound strategy is, perhaps, the most difficult piece of developing your campaign. It requires the development of a strategy to accomplish your stated outcome.

Remembering that we have to KNOW WHAT WORKS brings us to the development of STRATEGY. For the less experienced, this word and concept are often confused with CHANNELS or TACTICS. But strategy is not to be equated with tactics. Strategy is reality-based thinking. It is more about the "Why" and asks the question, "Why will people respond to my stated outcome?" Tactics is more about the "How" and asks the question, "What proven channels will enable people to best respond to my strategy?"

Developing sound strategy is where most integrated multichannel campaigns succeed or fail. To help you in developing a strategy for success, keep in mind that every strategy involves a STRONG OFFER (i.e., what are we asking our donors to do?). All of the advertisers for the consumer products I mentioned at the beginning of this rule know the value of a strong offer. For our purposes, the word "offer" has a very specific meaning. Here, an offer means we are answering five critical questions that apply to ALL channels used:

1. What will it cost to seize this opportunity or solve the problem?
2. What opportunity or problem is my ministry trying to seize or solve? (This is your outcome.)

3. What is my ministry doing to seize or solve?
4. How will the donor's gift seize or solve?
5. Why should the donor give now?

A sound strategy is also based upon the proven use of appropriate channels for each aspect of our campaign. Both of these words are critical. If our fundraising outcome is to raise $500,000, then the word "proven" means we know our strategy will work because we've done it before in a very similar context. In the absence of our own experience, we will need to rely upon trusted peers or counsel who have had success and can document their strategy and results conclusively. The word appropriate in this context implies we have either experienced success using this channel or, again, rely upon trusted peers or counsel who have experienced success with this channel. A word of caution here, there are many variables in any campaign. Overlooking, missing or ignoring any of them would be very detrimental to the success of the campaign.

STEP #5:

Matching our available channels to our strategy. Since, in our example, our fundraising outcome is to raise $500,000, it will likely involve a "seed gift" or matching corpus from major donor(s) and/or foundations. For our purposes, let's say we ask for $250,000 to be matched dollar for dollar.

If your ministry has an actively cultivated direct mail donor base of 15,000 supporters who have given within the past 12 months, AND 20% of your supporters who gave $100.00 or more as their largest single gift in the same

12-month period, you should expect a significant portion of the match to be raised from this channel. My proven experience says a follow-up direct mail appeal informing donors that there is still time to have their gift matched, or to make an additional gift, should raise about 50% of the initial matching gift appeal.

Printed and e-newsletters should carry articles carefully written and designed to coincide with all other channels being utilized in your campaign. Both of these channels should provide the opportunity to give and direct your readers to a campaign-dedicated landing page on your website.

The direct mail appeals should have digital support by email and mobile numbers (for donors with email addresses and mobile numbers), and your website should carry corresponding artwork and donate buttons that lead your donors to the landing page for the matching gift opportunity. Social media, again with corresponding artwork and offers, should support this same matching gift offer.

All of these channels, when fully integrated in their offer, message, style and look, will contribute to achieving your fundraising outcome. But (small word preceding a critical point), NOT ALL CHANNELS WILL PERFORM AT THE SAME LEVEL. The high-performing channels in this campaign will be your major donors and direct mail. All the other channels employed will contribute some direct income and increase response to your direct mail channels.

In this campaign example, the other channels I've identified above (but not utilized) are not likely to have much impact on achieving your fundraising outcome.

STEP #6:

Ensure integration. You will not only want to integrate the elements of this specific campaign, but you will also want to integrate this campaign with all other communications and fundraising activities that are scheduled to occur within your ministry. Full integration can be accomplished by developing and using a ministry-wide communications and fundraising calendar. This will assist you in coordinating your campaign without jeopardizing other critical initiatives.

Rule #38: *Madison Avenue is right! (multichannel = market penetration)* is becoming increasingly important to the effective fundraiser. Market penetration is simply shorthand for saying, "Making certain that everyone who cares about your mission, or might care, has had every available and affordable opportunity to hear and respond to your offer."

I hope this helps as you seek to use all the Master has entrusted to you to maximize the return and hear the encouraging words, "Well done, good and faithful servant."

RULE #39
"Speed counts!"

This rule is one that I actually enjoy. Anybody who really knows me wouldn't be surprised by this at all. I'm always in a hurry! If I could, I'd have everything done yesterday! Maybe that's why I like Jimmy John's™ TV and radio commercials. They are a Chicago-based sandwich company that makes great food. If you're familiar with them, you've likely been exposed to their commercials, the ones that say, "We deliver FREAKY FAST™!" One of their TV spots features an elderly man, sitting in his easy chair with a TV tray in front of him. He despondently looks at his traditional TV dinner, picks it up and throws it over his right shoulder. Reaching for the phone, he dials and says, "Hello, Jimmy John's™?" The very next moment his doorbell rings, the old man hollers, "C'mon in!" And, as the door opens, the Jimmy John's™ deliveryman is leaning against the doorpost! He says with a smile, "Jimmy John's™!" A voice-over says, "FREAKY FAST!™"

Maybe it's because I eat a lot of room service; I don't know. But it feels like it's every person's dream to have instant gratification, especially when you're hungry. I'm used to hearing room service or maybe even the pizza guy say, "That'll be to you within an hour..." I immediately look at my watch and grab a mozzarella stick out of the small fridge in my hotel room.

I absolutely LOVE it when someone exceeds my expectations! And I don't think I'm alone in this. Your donors are the same way. They LOVE promptness and accuracy! In *The Rules of Fundraising,* I spent quite a bit of time on the importance of processing and mailing donor thank-you letters back to your supporters within 24-48 hours. This is to exceed expectations and to give them something in their hands to be able to give your ministry yet another gift. Speed is critical here. It tells the donor you are thankful and prompt. It also thanks them before another solicitation arrives. This is exactly why I discourage online receipting. Yes, it is faster than snail mail, but traditional, 1st-class mail is MUCH more effective in obtaining "bounce-back" or thank-you letter gifts. It's this fundraiser's experience that using 3rd-class postage is slower and much of the mail is never delivered. The end result is less speed for your thank-you letter and sometimes (about a third of the time, according to postal watchdog groups), no 3rd-class letter is delivered at all! Let's face it, when a donor has to make the decision between giving to two equally wonderful causes, a prompt thank you tilts the scales in your favor.

Employing the FREAKY FAST approach to all other aspects of donor-initiated communication will help to instill in donors that you know them and that you care. When a donor takes the time to telephone your ministry, what do they hear? Is it a recorded message that sends them all over the universe pressing buttons to finally reach the message, "Hello, you've reached Joe in the Development Office. I can't take your call right now, but every call is important, so please leave a message after the tone"?

Having worked as the Vice President of Resource Development for a nonprofit, I found it helpful to establish a direct line for donors to call that was answered in the Development Department. During office hours we made certain that donors could always have quick and easy access to a listening, caring human being.

Several years ago, I was particularly pleased to walk into a ministry and hear their receptionist answer the phone, "Good afternoon, this is [ministry name], how can I serve you?" I was so impressed with the attitude of service that I've adopted the same approach for my own company. If you call during business hours you should have a friendly voice answer and say, "Douglas Shaw & Associates, how may I serve you?" Fast, personal, friendly and welcoming are all part of the rule that *Speed counts!*

NOTES:

RULE #40
"Your donors need to know what their giving has accomplished."

I was raised by a family of hillbillies. No, they didn't capture me in the parking lot at a rib-eating contest—these folks were my biological family. At first I didn't appreciate this unique culture (especially in 8th grade when my thrift store clothes were...let's say a little different from my classmates). But as I've grown older, I've begun to appreciate the humility and simplicity that my heritage provided me. Now I often find great richness in the culture and language. Expressions like, "Now that dog won't hunt!" is a very country way of saying, "I don't trust what I just heard." To me, it has an illustrative quality to it that describes a culture that was filled with "coon hounds" like blue ticks and black and tans. Noisy dogs all with tails that could sweep you off your feet, lacerated ears from encounters with raccoon and possum that just wanted to be left alone, were trophies of the chase. In my early culture, a dog that wouldn't hunt was deemed pretty worthless and certainly not to be trusted.

Trust is what a donor is looking for too. When they entrust their gift to your ministry, they expect that you are going to use it as you promised. Let me say this again but this time a little differently. When a donor gives to you, they "hope" you are going to use their donation as you represented it in your communication to them.

In my flying about North America, I encounter fellow travelers who often ask me what I do for a living. When I tell them, "I'm a fundraising consultant," I can usually predict their next question. "My husband and I support so and so. Do you know anything about them? Are they a good organization?" I've found that donors are constantly looking for assurance. A little deeper into the conversation, I'll usually hear, "There are so many scams out there; I just want to make sure we're giving where it's going to do the most good."

There ARE a lot of scams out there. Because most of us in ministry are on the up-and-up, perhaps we don't realize just how much this question is on the minds of most donors. Now that older people are spending more time online, their fears are reinforced every time they pick up a virus or encounter an email from some developing country where the initiator has tons of loot that is frozen in some account and they just need a little help from a friendly soul to release the funds to their family here in North America. For just a small fee, say $300, a permit can be obtained to free up a vast fortune, a portion of which the initiator will certainly share with the friendly soul once the transaction is complete. Sound familiar?

And who hasn't heard or read about some well-known organization that has discovered malfeasance on the part of the CEO, who is now serving time for embezzlement? All of this is having a significant impact on philanthropy today.

But, in this fundraiser's mind, all of this can be overcome if we just do what we can and should be doing in the first place, i.e., providing donors with positive feedback about the good works their gifts are doing to save and change lives. There are so very many ways available to us today, that providing a supporter with affirmation of their giving should be relatively easy. Here are just a few ideas that come to mind:

- A thank-you letter that accompanies your receipt and bounce-back document (we've already addressed this earlier)
- A printed newsletter, which focuses on the donor and all the good that's been accomplished in the past few weeks through their generosity (by the way, you can package this newsletter in such a way that it raises significant additional funds—see *The Rules of Fundraising*)
- An online version of this same newsletter formatted for email and smartphone rather than print (just don't expect to receive much income from this channel)
- A thank-you phone call that does NOT ask for a gift, but DOES report on the impact of the ministry you and your supporter are committed to
- A receipt stuffer that accompanies your receipt and thank-you letter that is a simple 7" X 10" front and back newsletter
- A "thank you" section featured in a prominent place on the home page of your website
- An annual report that provides an overview of the entire ministry (this too is packaged for response and will at minimum pay for itself and most likely generate additional income)

- A small group dinner or dessert for major donors that serves as a "ministry update" presented by your CEO or board members. Since this does NOT involve an "ask," most board members are very willing to oblige this kind of request. This is, indeed, a great way to involve board members.
- A major donor weekend event that is 90% thanking and reporting and 10% asking for a donation or faith-promise pledge
- An assuring endorsement by a trusted and prominent donor in your community, state or country featured in any or all of the communication channels above

Constant assurance for your supporters will increase your donor retention rates, grow your donor file and bless those who feel led to use what God has given them to support your mission. That's why this rule exists: *Your donors need to know what their giving has accomplished!*

RULE #41
"Technology can be your friend and your enemy."

I'm hardly qualified to write about the intricacies of using technology (just ask my wife, Kathryn, or my millennial children). But thoughtful use of basic technology is essential in just about any field, especially philanthropy, where we are always committed to informing donors that we know them and care about them. Here we'll examine some of the great benefits associated with responsibly using technology and the terrible pitfalls of doing things poorly.

Back in the dark ages (the 1970s) when I was attending seminary, my peers and I couldn't wait for each new issue of a Christian satire magazine called, The Wittenberg Door™, to land in our mailboxes. We salivated in anticipation of the arrival of each issue. Our favorite section was "Truth Is Stranger Than Fiction." We just couldn't wait to see who was going to be lampooned next!

The feature that comes to mind while writing about this rule, "Technology can be your friend AND your enemy," made me laugh to the point of tears. But I assure you, the ministry featured wasn't laughing. It was a personalized fundraising letter:

Chicken Take O.
123 Anystreet
Anytown, USA

"Dear Chicken...

I am personally very grateful for your Faith Partner Commitment.

Because you and other friends answered my plea, Chicken, I now believe we will be able to keep [ministry name] on nearly all our present stations.

I know this is a joy to you personally, and I hope you will join me in prayer that we will now use this opportunity to bring others in your community—and across the nation—to a saving faith in Jesus Christ.

Each time you join me for a broadcast, I think you should take great pride in knowing it is YOUR Faith Partner Commitment which is helping to make the program possible.

As I promised, Chicken, each month I'm going to write you a letter such as this discussing the controversial issues of our time—and this month I want to talk to you about" ...

The yolk was clearly on them!

The personal letter to Chicken Take O. was both an overuse and unintended abuse of data. It could have been avoided if organizations, churches, foundations, corporations and the like had been suppressed during the data selection process, leaving only individuals for solicitation.

Many years later, when a company I worked for at the time made a mistake in personalizing a letter, it wasn't quite so funny. Their letter began:

"Dear <Salutation>!" It was supposed to read something like:

"Dear Mrs. Smith," or "Dear Mr. Jones," but the salutation data field was never populated. It had gotten past my employer's data folks, the proofreader, my own personal review, and the ministry staff...until it arrived in the ministry's mailbox, that is!

I received a very distressed phone call from the Vice President of Development,

"Douglas Shaw!"

"Yes?"

"I opened this month's fundraising letter just now, and I'm furious!"

"What's the matter?" I asked, holding my breath.

"My letter begins, 'Dear Salutation!' You're going to pay for this entire letter, Doug Shaw!" ...not the words you want to hear from a beloved client.

Now, we all make mistakes. But this one was a biggie! It embarrassed the Vice President, the CEO, the board and the entire ministry; this was clearly not our intent. But the biggest concern was the impact it might have on the very donors who loved and supported this great organization. I'll tell you the rest of the story in a minute...

As you know, technology is the very life's blood of direct response fundraising. Using it strategically can increase your income exponentially. The combined effect of selecting the right donors for the right message at the right time can only be enhanced when donors are presented with the right "offer" and gift arrays that match each individual donor's giving pattern. When ALL of the data is carefully selected and extracted from your database with precision and accuracy, it becomes what I call appropriate data.

Appropriate data is the circuitry that wires together all the components of successful direct response fundraising communication. This rule: "Technology can be your friend AND your enemy," is focused largely upon the use or abuse of this circuitry.

Handled correctly, technology can help to increase donations by building donors into our fundraising appeals, regardless of what channel is used. With all of the technology available to us today, we can ask a specific donor for a relevant gift for something we KNOW they have already supported at the time of year they have demonstrated through their previous giving.

Now...back to my own data foul-up:

The "Dear Salutation" incident was clearly a mistake. It is a common error that keeps development officers (and fundraising consultants) awake at night, staring at the ceiling, wondering if they'll have a job in the morning. Here's how the vice president and I finished our conversation...

"Could I ask you a question?" I asked gingerly.

"What?" she replied.

I chose my words VERY carefully now. "Can we wait and see how this appeal performs? If it doesn't make its intended income forecast, I promise our company will make things right."

"Okay...we'll wait...but I know this mailing is going to flop!"

As it turned out, the appeal exceeded its financial forecast! I was as surprised as anyone! The generous response by this ministry's donors was just another example of God's grace. It didn't excuse the mistake, but thankfully the ministry wasn't punished for my employer's technology error.

While I encourage all of us to rely on God's grace, I also encourage careful proofreading, especially where donor personalization is used to inform donors that we know them, how much they like to give, what they choose to support and when they give.

Lastly, no discussion of this rule would be complete without addressing the high importance of maintaining "data hygiene." If we desire to communicate to our donors that we know them, it requires diligence in maintaining clean and up-to-date information in our database. I can't count the number of times that ministries have been taken to task for sending appeals to donors who are now deceased, divorced or have married and therefore made a change to their name.

So how do we know when these changes occur? It's time-consuming, but one of the most helpful ways to know of changes is to take great care in reading any notes that are written on direct mail or newsletter reply devices. Often, if a reply device is mailed back to a ministry without a gift, it is sorted into a pile for processing "later." Here's the problem: often "later" never comes, or it comes much too late.

If we truly want to have technology be our friend, rather than our enemy, we will be well advised to be vigilant in carefully reading and responding to ANY written requests on donor reply devices. As we saw in Rule #39, *Speed counts...* here too! It is highly likely that someone in your organization is running a data select right now. You and your ministry will be best served if your donor information is kept completely up to date.

Another area to monitor deceased donors is through close communication with those processing bequests in your organization. Bequests are usually a cause for financial celebration. But there is valuable information here for those who want to treat survivors with respect. For local or regional ministries, scanning obituaries can also provide helpful information that can be used to keep your data up to date.

Name changes are sensitive areas. People normally do not change their names unless they need to. There is most likely an important event that has brought this request for change. Divorce, for example, is always a highly emotional event that can leave a participant anxious to move on. Having their name changed quickly is very important to them. A marriage most often comes with a name change too, and a prompt response to a request here is equally important in helping a donor feel heard. Anyone who has gone through the journey of requesting that their name be changed because of marriage can attest to the lengthy and often frustrating process this can be. This is an excellent opportunity for you to prove to your donors that you are listening to them.

All of the above are intended to demonstrate the truth of this rule: *"Technology can be your friend and your enemy!"* You and your donors will be served best when technology is embraced as your friend.

RULE #42
"Be careful what you ask for... you just might get it!"

In Western, English-speaking cultures, the phrase, "Be careful what you ask for...you just might get it," is usually offered as a word of caution. The context for someone saying this is usually based in their concern for a friend or colleague who is articulating their desire for something that may have unexpected consequences.

This fundraising rule has to do with helping you to fully understand what you REALLY want a donor to do. While it relates the preceding rule, it also creates a framework for thinking through who to contact, what to tell them, how to approach them and how to determine how much money to ask for. A well-constructed offer is essential (see *The Rules of Fundraising*, Rule #8). In case you haven't seen *The Rules of Fundraising*, I'll recap the Five Critical Components of an Effective Offer here and then move on to new insights:

THE FIVE CRITICAL COMPONENTS OF AN EFFECTIVE OFFER

1. What is the problem or opportunity your organization is trying to solve? e.g., People are dying due to lack of food.
2. What is your organization planning to do to solve the

problem or seize the opportunity? e.g., Food is available, and distribution channels are in place.

3. How much money does your organization need to solve the problem or seize the opportunity? e.g., Provide the total cost to buy the food and distribute it.

4. Tell your donors how their gifts will solve the problem or help you take full advantage of the opportunity. e.g., You can feed one person for $6.00 per day (using your own real numbers, of course).

5. Tell your donors why it is important for them to give today! e.g. XX,XXX people in your area go to bed hungry every night.

I've known enough organizations, throughout the years, that have NOT followed rule number 8 that it makes me want to fly over every ministry in the world and drop leaflets saying, "Remember The Five Critical Components of an Effective Offer!" Way too many great organizations draft letters, emails, create radio spots or even hold major donor events that do everything but ask for a gift! People ask for prayer...and they get it, they ask for people to pray about what God would have them do...and their donors pray, but few respond with a gift. But when a ministry asks for an appropriate gift, using the Five Critical Components of an Effective Offer, they usually get what they ask for!

There's a sad but true story that circulates in the halls of direct response fundraisers. It's called the "Dollar Story." It involves a direct response agency that developed a direct mail package with a dollar bill showing through the window of an envelope. The intended idea was that by giving the potential donor a dollar and asking them to send it back, along with their own dollar, the potential donor would become an active donor. Unfortunately, as the story goes, very few, if anybody, responded. The recipients of this mailing just kept the money. You have to also wonder if a few mail carriers made a few extra bucks along the way too! Here's the really sad part of this story...they thought this would be so successful that they mailed 1 million packages!!!

Envision a group of development people sitting around a conference table at their ministry. Somebody says, "You know, we have 40,000 active donors on our mailing list. If everybody would just give $1.00, we could fund this project!"

On the face of it, this sounds like a good idea; after all, the donors have already proven their caring for your cause by giving to your ministry. Most of them have given more than $1.00, so this should be a slam dunk! The only problem is that there are those, sometimes irritating, inviolate, rules in fundraising. Let's see what would likely happen if you attempted this well-meaning strategy:

1. A person who gives an average gift of $500 sends you a gift of $1.00.
2. A person who usually sends in $20.00 sends you $1.00
3. You don't receive 100% response like you had hoped, rather you receive about a 7% response (which is generally pretty good for most mailings).
4. So, instead of receiving the hoped-for $40,000, you receive $2,800 or 7% of 40,000 donors.
5. Assuming your mailing was sent all 3rd-class mail, at a package cost of $0.85, the whole effort cost you

$34,000. You achieved a loss of $31,200 for all your efforts...

So be careful what you ask for...you just might get it!

But let's look at a few things that can help you immensely in asking for what you really want from a donor:

1. SEGMENT YOUR DONOR FILE INTO SEVERAL CATEGORIES:
- Active donors (people who have given a gift of any size within the last 12 months)
- Newly acquired donors (people who have given their very first gift within the last 12 months)
- Lapsed donors (people who have given in the past but NOT within the last 13 months)
- Non-donors (people on your mailing list who have never given)

Now, I've found that writing a version of an appeal letter (modifying the format for each channel used, e.g., email or mobile) for each segment being communicated with greatly enhances the likelihood of response. The recipient feels better when they are communicated with in a way that proves you know a little about them, i.e., they are committed givers, new givers, they haven't given in a while, or they have never given.

2. DETERMINE YOUR GIFT ARRAYS:
Since people will normally give according to their giving pattern, and if you use the Five Critical Components of an Effective Offer, you might create your gift arrays as follows:

If the donor's last gift was:	Then you might ask for:			
$.01-9.99	[ ]$15	[ ]$10	[ ]$20	[ ]$____
$10-14.99	[ ]$20	[ ]$15	[ ]$25	[ ]$____
$15-24.99	[ ]$30	[ ]$25	[ ]$35	[ ]$____
$25-49.99	[ ]$50	[ ]$35	[ ]$65	[ ]$____
$50-99.99	[ ]$90	[ ]$75	[ ]$100	[ ]$____
$100-249.99	[ ]$225	[ ]$150	[ ]$275	[ ]$____
$250+	[ ]$____			

By the way, I do indeed realize that the gift amounts are out of order. In fact they are intentionally structured this way. Let me explain...

- If a donor is reading the gift-giving options on a reply device, they often mark the first box (which would be an automatic upgrade over their last gift).
- In addition, when a donor begins to scan the giving options, they see that the second gift amount is lower than the first amount, and it encourages them to take the time to read the third amount.
- All of this is designed to engage the reader and give them more reason to consider what gift they can give.
- The $____ is included in all giving arrays to allow space for the donor who wants to give something other than what was suggested to them. Many folks, like me, don't like being told what to do. I don't know their motives, but for me it's some kind of authority issue or something...
- There is, after all, no reason to lose a gift because we didn't give them a place to express themselves.
- Using only the $____ for every donor whose last gift

was $250 or more is intended to free up the donor to write as large a gift as they would like. Oftentimes a donor who has given a gift of $250 has the ability to give $1,000 or more.

An even better use of **The Five Critical Components of an Effective Offer** is to tailor your gift arrays to the specific nature of your offer, e.g.:

If the donor's <u>last</u> gift was: $.01-9.99

Then you might ask for: [ ] $12 will provide two hungry people with food for a day
[ ] $6 will care for a hungry person for an entire day
[ ] $18 will help three people to have enough to eat for a day
[ ] $＿＿ to help as many people as you can

You get the idea, and can build the remainder of your gift arrays based upon the metrics of your specific offer.

By crafting your offers carefully and thoughtfully, you can significantly increase giving from your donors, lapsed donors, new donors and non-donors. That's why this rule states: *"Be careful what you ask for...you just might get it!"* Again, it's a word of caution from one fundraiser to another so you can maximize your income and minimize *unexpected consequences!*

RULE #43
"You can't over-communicate... or can you?"

In 1980 BPC (before personal computers), I often found that not-for-profits were in danger of under-communicating to their donors. In fact, I still run into this with more historic organizations today. Traditions do die hard...

Once Al Gore introduced us to www (World Wide Web), things began to shift. Today, it seems like anyone can send email blasts to everybody all the time! We call this SPAM (which I personally think does disservice to the gelatinous canned meat that I consumed and hated as a child).

You know SPAMMERS. They're the modern-day version of people who used to send those terrible Christmas family newsletters. Remember? They were the letters where little Jennifer has just received her Ph.D. in astrophysics and Lance Jr. has just been named Supreme Court Justice. Hubby has been nominated for the Nobel Peace Prize, and Mom (usually the author of this self-esteem crushing stuff) has just won a Martha Stewart Award for making a replica of the Eiffel Tower out of a wire coat hanger.

Well today you don't have to wait for the letter carrier to receive this precious holiday reminder that yet another year has gone by and you still haven't lost any weight. Today all you have to do is turn on your laptop, iPad, iPhone or any number of electronic devices that must be turned off once the aircraft door has been closed. There are the unwanted messages...just waiting for you! Useless information about something you started receiving three years ago because in a moment of trying to increase your social media footprint you stepped in it. And it won't come off your shoe, or your screen in this case, and the blue unsubscribe link seldom works. In my mind it's really just a tease to remind you that you're forever in the clutches of AN OVER-COMMUNICATOR!

Okay, so maybe I haven't yet mastered all the protective elements of technology, but I don't think I'm alone on this. If most of your donors are aged 55 and older, chances are pretty good that they too have technical tangles when it comes to cutting their way free from the unwanted aspects of the worldwide web.

Sooooo, I've found that I appreciate a person or an organization that has found just the right balance in their communication mix. Not too much, not too little, and always something that I, the donor, am interested in. Kind of a tall order, huh?

Here's a little analytical tool that I picked up along the way to help me in a situation like this. Perhaps it'll help you too.

1.   What is reality? In this context that may mean, "How much contact are we, as a ministry, having with our donors?"

- Emails (by department)
- Direct mail appeals
- Thank-you letters
- Newsletters

- Phone calls
- Personal visits
- Planned giving newsletters
- Volunteer opportunities
- Invitations to special events

You get the idea.

2.   Just plot out the number of contacts from all sources within your organization, and write it on a calendar.

3.   Look for overlaps in communication.

4.   Place yourself in the role of your donor to determine how it would feel to receive all the communication your ENTIRE ORGANIZATION is sending.

5.   Monitor recent complaints from donors (notes on reply devices, emails, etc.).

6.   Now, get your team of communicators together and plot out what your most conservative donor would want to receive.

7.   Working together, stretch that conservative donor into a moderate, and you've likely struck a reasonable balance!

So let's take a look at what number 7 above would look like...

Representatives from PR, development (advancement, stewardship or whatever you call it), planned giving, publications, donor relations, alumni relations (you know, the whole gang), have a meeting. In fact, for some organizations, this may be the very first time they've sat in one room together. You might start the meeting by taking a mental note of who is sitting next to each other. This may be an indicator of how the meeting's going to go. Let's face it, each person present has her/his own agenda, budget, goals, etc., and every person is going to try and defend his/her turf. This is the reason you need a tiebreaker in the room; perhaps she's the Vice President of Advancement. It's been my experience that the meeting will be the most productive if the VP limits her role to that of listener and tiebreaker, that's it.

You will also need a master facilitator. This is someone who knows his role. They are there to help you accomplish your purpose, i.e., strike the right balance in the amount of communication to send to your donors/constituents. I've found it best if the facilitator is from another part of your organization so they can remove themselves from the outcome.

Did I mention that you should plan about four hours for this collaboration? Well I meant to. Anyway, it's going to take a great deal of time to reach consensus with so many varying interests represented.

A good facilitator begins a meeting like this by acknowledging all of the elephants in the room. They just get them out there, so everyone can acknowledge and hopefully state their interests. The facilitator will also make certain the purpose of the meeting is clearly understood; usually they'll have it in writing on a flipchart or whiteboard or projected onto a screen. This keeps your purpose in plain view and becomes a reference point during the meeting.

Each member of the team should come prepared with samples of their communication, any audience segmentation being used (like volunteers, major donors, planned giving constituents) and the current schedule for communicating to your audiences. The facilitator asks each member to articulate their purpose, goals, segmentation and the effectiveness of each channel of communication. As the meeting continues, it will become clear just how much information is being sent out from your organization as a whole. If my experience is any indicator, your donors/constituents might unintentionally be being deluged with stuff. Lots of stuff!

It's worth noting here that donors generally don't distinguish between your organization's departments. They just see everything as coming from your ministry.

The facilitator can help you to see the "log-jams," i.e., places where a donor/recipient receives several communications in the same month, week or even day! Over the years I've heard of donors receiving up to three communications (usually via the mailbox) **on the very same day.** This is when the complaints about too much mail start to roll in.

And this is why you will need a four-hour meeting...

The facilitator can help you not only better coordinate your communication channels, but also facilitate the collaboration that can reduce the flow of information without cutting any department off at the knees (e.g., the publications department can help by ensuring that every issue of your newsletter or magazine carries a planned giving article). Another helpful approach is to have your direct mail appeals carry a checkbox and a line that indicates: "I would like more information about including [your ministry name here] in my will." This may allow you to reduce your planned giving newsletters by an issue or two.

As this rule indicates, you CAN over-communicate. Coordinating and collaborating can help you and your ministry to become more balanced in your amount of communication, thereby preserving those precious donor/constituent relationships.

NOTES:

RULE #44
"If you build it, they will come. (capital campaign effects on annual giving)"

You don't have to be a baseball fan to have watched and enjoyed the 1989 film *Field of Dreams,* based upon W.P. Kinsella's book *Shoeless Joe.* It was filmed in and around Dubuque, Iowa, and it told the story of corn farmer Ray Kinsella (Kevin Costner) and his wife Annie (Amy Madigan), and their struggle to keep their farm. On several occasions while out in the yard, near the cornfield, Ray hears a voice, "If you build it, they will come." Over time he becomes convinced that he is supposed to build a lighted, professional-size baseball diamond. Even though he's financially struggling, he decides to obey the voice, and incredible things begin to happen. I won't tell you any more or how it ends, but you can buy the book or rent the movie if your curiosity has been tweaked. I'm not even a serious baseball fan, but I think it's worth watching, especially when compared to *Duck Dynasty.*

When a ministry decides to enter into a capital campaign, it's much the same as experienced by the character played by Kevin Costner. Someone, somewhere in the leadership of your ministry has heard God's voice, prompting them to build, expand or replace facilities or structures to increase the effectiveness of your ministry.

Capital campaign advisors (which I am not) will tell you that a new church building will increase your attendance. I don't know why this is true, but the same can be said of most of the rules of fundraising. The rules just exist, and I found it wise to follow them.

But having spent my life as a direct response fundraiser, using direct mail, digital, radio, newspaper ads (You remember newspapers, don't you? They were the things that commuters used to read.), etc., I can tell you that capital campaigns DO affect ongoing support for most ministries.

I can't tell you how many times I've been asked by nervous board members and CEOs, *"Now, just how much do you think our capital campaign will affect our ongoing support?"* I usually respond with something like, "Well, I hate to say it, but you could see as much as a 20% downturn in general fund giving." At least this is my experience. Others in the fundraising field may have a different number, but most likely you'll see a slump in your general fund support.

Fundraising craftsmen know the truth of this rule. Capital campaigns are good for your ministry, but there are side effects. I'm just encouraging you to read the label.

Campaigns demonstrate the vitality of your vision, mission and values. They can revitalize your ministry and certainly attract new donors. To me, and most likely to many of your donors, nothing says success like a completed campaign! It says you are growing, improving and providing essential services. A completed campaign also shouts that you have people of means who believe you are worthy of support.

There are many outstanding capital campaign firms who

are both highly competent and in alignment with your values. Let me encourage you to tell them of your concerns about annual fund losses during your campaign. Any reputable firm will take this into consideration and likely build an operating fund component into your campaign. By this I'm referring to the funds necessary to operate your new facility for a few years. This can be a great relief to board members, CEOs and development officers who are rightly concerned about the impact of your campaign on your annual fund. As this rule states, *If you build it, they will come.* Hopefully this will encourage you to plan for the impact of a campaign on your day-to-day funding needs and enable you to soar!

NOTES:

RULE #45
"Changing the channel can cause you to lose your audience."

I remember lying on the floor of our little cabin when I was growing up, trying to watch our old Zenith black-and-white television through a blinding snowstorm of static and poor signal. This was long before cable or satellite TV, and every house with a television sported an antenna on its roof. Every house but ours, that is. We were the proud owners of a special antenna system; very few people had the privilege of using one.

Now, the coat hanger sticking out of the top of our TV had to be positioned just right to bring in an adequate signal. My dad had supercharged ours by carefully wrapping tinfoil on the upside down metal coat hanger to enhance its effectiveness. My job was to stand beside the TV and turn the hanger slowly until my dad yelled, "Stop! That's it!" Then I'd carefully release my fingers from the hanger, back carefully away from the TV, and then flop back down onto the rug and watch the show. If memory serves, there were four channels in our Maple Valley, Washington, cabin—channels 2, 4, 5 and UHF for Ultra High Frequency. Our special system could pick up sound or sight on the UHF channel, but never both at the same time. It's hardly worth noting that we didn't turn the dial to this channel except by accident.

It was here, lying on the floor, that I was introduced to *The Ed Sullivan Show, The Honeymooners,* and on Friday nights, *"The Friday Night Fights,* brought to you by Gillette!" Da Dat Da, Da da da da Da, the theme song was insidiously branded into my young mind. Dad would sit on the edge of the couch and tell me the stats of all the fighters. On special nights, he'd say, "This ought to be a good one!" while rubbing his calloused hands together in anticipation.

I don't know exactly when it happened. But the consequences were severe. Sometime during my youth, the *Friday Night Fights* just disappeared! No more Gillette, no more theme song and no more Channel 5. Once the fights were gone, so were we.

Some well-meaning TV executives sat in a room in New York City and decided what we should watch on Friday nights. They didn't ask us. They didn't even tell us they weren't going to ask us. They just decided. So we changed the channel and watched the *Ted Mack Amateur Hour* (yesteryear's version of *American Idol)* on Channel 4.

As fundraisers, we may unknowingly be doing the same thing to our audiences. A donor may have gone to our website, checked us out and made a decision to click one of the "GIVE NOW" buttons. We receive their gift, send them a thank-you letter with a return envelope, and add them to our direct mail stream. From then on, we mail to them at least once a month and wonder why they have such a low response to our mailings.

With all of the emphasis being given to online communication today, the reverse approach is more often the case. A prospect may respond to one of our donor acquisition mailings. We enter the data, send them a thank-you letter and receipt with a return envelope. From then on, if we have their email address, we only send them email blasts because it's cheaper.

In both cases, we changed the channel on the donor, without asking them. The donor becomes a lapsed donor and we attempt to reactivate them with little response. They start giving to another worthy cause.

The good news in all of this is that we have better information than the New York TV executives. We can determine which channel a first-time donor used to give to our ministry. We can respond to them without changing the channel.

By carefully monitoring the channel or channels donors use to support our cause, we can develop fundraising strategies that are based upon their giving patterns as opposed to our *decisions*. Observing donor behavior allows us to "turn the hanger" in just the right way to give them the best reception to our messaging.

I think it's important to add something here. I'm not trying to make the case against direct mail. There's already too much of this going on today. In fact, I LOVE direct mail...because, when done correctly, it works! To this old fundraiser, direct mail is still the crescent wrench in my fundraising toolbox. It's easily adjustable and will fit almost every donor, lapsed donor or prospect in some way.

At the risk of sounding inconsistent, let me cite Rule #33 from my first book: *The rules of fundraising are sometimes applicable and sometimes not...that's why it can be helpful to have a guide.* This rule hinges upon the context of the rule and learning the variables in fundraising.

Here's the variable in this scenario: Most donors like to receive direct mail if...it's from a cause they believe in and if... it is written in a way that is appropriate for their relationship with your organization. At our fundraising consulting firm, Douglas Shaw & Associates, we represent over 30 ministries. We're seeing more and more direct mail donors receiving a direct mail appeal, reading it and responding online. This change in behavior isn't being done by tens of thousands of donors, mind you, but the numbers of multichannel donors is increasing, and this is a good thing.

Multichannel donors make the best donors (The Rules of Fundraising, Rule #29). By way of recap, in the event that you haven't read my first set of rules, here are the results of a study done for one of our most long-standing client partners (as well as borne out by other industry research and client experience):

- Approximately 92% of all donations are from offline channels
- So about 8% of all donations are from online channels
- The average value of a donor from offline is $398.00
- The average from an online donor is $345.00
- The average from a multichannel donor is $958.00

We have seen this pattern consistently across the ministries we represent. *This is the variable in this scenario.*

Now, how do we put all of this info together? When a new donor's first gift is given online, it's a good idea to continue with online communication **and** direct mail appeals (if we've acquired their physical address). We've also had excellent success with response to snail mail sent to online donors...*they just respond online rather than through the postal system.* I've found that response from online donors is lower when all they receive is an online appeal. Sending them direct mail appeals "drives" them to our website or micro-site, which can be established for a specific appeal.

I know I'm not alone in experiencing that outright and unannounced changing of the channel can cause you to lose your audience, but you can *add* channels and significantly increase response as noted in the bullet points above.

So as this rule states, *Changing the channel can cause you to lose your audience.*

NOTES:

RULE #46
"It takes two gifts to make a donor."

It's part of what's called "The Horn of Africa" because of its geographical shape in North East Africa. The year was 1983, and famine swept through Ethiopia. I was working in the fundraising department at World Relief, a faith-based relief and development organization. The 1983-85 famine would go down as the worst famine in Ethiopia in over 100 years. Before it was over, more than 400,000 people would lose their lives to the effects surrounding starvation.

My job was to help raise funding to match government and U.N. funding that was being channeled through non-governmental organizations, or NGOs, as they're called. The political tensions in the area had contributed heavily to the circumstances leading into the famine itself, so the private sector became a critical force in the channeling of funds and the resulting lifesaving assistance. Local governments were suspected of using food distribution for political gain.

At that time the whole world was watching as the media seized upon this horror, and what Abraham Lincoln termed "the better angels of our nature" resulted in billions of dollars of aid being poured into this agonizing nation and region. Every NGO in the world involved in emergency aid was raising money to assist. This was my baptism by fire as a new fundraiser.

Times like this are when I believe the media is at its best. Sitting in our living rooms and at our dining room tables, we saw the effects of prolonged malnutrition on children with reddish hair and distended bellies, the calling cards of starvation.

Raising money for the Ethiopian famine was buoyed by the constant media coverage. All of us involved used every communication channel available to get the word out, and thankfully generosity prevailed.

As an emerging fundraiser, I saw the opportunity to acquire thousands of new donors. The response was both gratifying and the volume overwhelming; as you know, both feelings are far too infrequent in the trenches of fundraising. But seize the opportunity we did, and countless lives were saved as a result of the generosity of those who lived in much more comfortable circumstances.

All of us involved in the funding effort were expecting great things from those responding to the famine. None of us were prepared for the disappointment that was to follow…

It's likely that billions of dollars were spent in attempts to convert famine donors into ongoing relief and development supporters. But try as we might, we fundraisers learned an essential lesson: *a disaster donation does not equate to a mission-driven donation.* Furthermore, we learned that a single gift from a new donor did not necessarily translate into continued giving. It was with great disappointment that I learned the reality of this harsh rule: "It Takes Two Gifts to Make a Donor." "Why?" I continued to ask. "If a person is moved to make a gift through donor acquisition efforts, why doesn't the same person respond like existing committed donors do?"

Hopefully, my experience can be of service to you. What I've come to experience and believe has to do with human behavior. We like to try things out, fix things and then move on to some other media-supported catastrophe, unless we're given highly compelling incentives to re-engage financially.

If it's true that the number one reason people give is belief in the mission of your organization, and I believe it is, this can serve us all well. It can inform any second gift strategy that we develop.

I recently spoke with two top direct response strategists. I put the same question to each of them in separate interviews. Here's a summation of what each had to say:

Wiley Stinnett, Senior Vice President and Executive Creative Director:

"Send a thank-you letter sooner rather than later. The longer it takes for a donor to receive an acknowledgement of their first gift, the less likely a second gift will be forthcoming.

"There is a raging debate about whether or not to use a new donor welcome series. I have found that just including first-time donors into your regular donor cultivation mailings works better. The research I've read says the same things; put your new donors straight into your active donor file mail stream.

"Due to the time when data is selected, it could take 4-6

weeks before new donors are even selected for mailings. If the segmentation strategy being used doesn't include donors giving at a lower level (most first gifts are indeed smaller), it could be 3-4 months before a new donor begins to receive mail.

"New donors are like fish, they're best when fresh and stink when they are too old.

"Many ministries decide to hold off on asking first-time donors for a second gift, because they don't want to bother them. The best time to get a second gift is right after the first gift! But make certain that the new donor has received a thank-you letter for their first gift before you ask for the second one.

"The absolute BEST way to obtain a second gift is to use every channel available, e.g., direct mail, send a text message that chases or immediately follows the second letter itself, and then be certain the new donor is included in all other digital channels as well."

<u>Mark Loux, A colleague and third generation fundraiser</u>:

"There are two things that are critical: timing and specific acknowledgement (i.e., the thank-you letter thanks them for the specific nature of their gift rather than a generic thank-you letter).

"Make a *thank-you* phone call right away. This should be a thank-you call only. Not a call soliciting a gift. It's also a good practice to ask them if you can pray for them. This changes the dynamics of your relationship with the new donor; it's no longer transactional but real. You can also ask them if there's anything else they might need from your ministry. It often leaves the new donor thinking, 'Really? They just called to thank me?'

"Give them the opportunity to give to the same thing they gave to with their first gift.

"The important thing is relationship, e.g., if they gave to help with the earthquake in Haiti, make their second request something related, like a request for your ministry's ongoing work in Haiti."

Both of my esteemed colleagues stress the importance of immediacy in asking for a second gift. Time is of the utmost importance when a person entrusts their first gift to your ministry. Send them a very specific thank-you letter within 24-48 hours, and then ask them for a second gift right away.

Let's revisit the Ethiopian famine of 1983 for a moment. What have we learned about disaster-related gifts? Crises like Hurricane Katrina, the earthquakes in Haiti and Nepal, as well as the more recent Ebola outbreak in West Africa, all have brought many new donors into the ministries serving in these areas. But what have these new donors done?

In many ways a disaster donor is an *event* donor rather than a mission-based donor. Once the event has passed, the donations cease. My esteemed colleagues and I have seen this dynamic, time and again. Second donations come from people who come to understand your reason for being, your mission. They believe in who you are, what you believe and what you do. The greatest likelihood of second gifts and ongoing support is also going to be determined by how you treat a donor upon receipt of their first gift and every one thereafter. This is why we've come to believe and teach the rule, *"It takes two gifts to make a donor."*

RULE #47
"Old friends are better than new friends or even no friends..."

A few years ago, I was on a business trip that took me to Northern California. My flight required that I land in Sacramento, where an old college and seminary friend was now pastoring a church. I couldn't wait to see Ron and his wife Kathleen. We had met at Simpson College, when it was still based in the city of San Francisco. Since we were both married, and there wasn't any married student housing at Simpson College, Ron and I both lived off campus. This gave us many opportunities to spend evenings together exploring the less expensive, college student type activities of this amazing city. Since Ron was a Northern California native, he was also able to introduce me to many adventures in the Sierra Nevada Mountains near his childhood home of Sonora. We had shared so many good times together over a period of about eight years, including working together painting houses as a way of paying for our seminary tuition. So we are and will be friends for life.

A friendship like this is a gift indeed. You know what it's like. You may not see this kind of friend for a long time, but when you do get together, you just pick up where you left off. There's nothing like it! A bond exists that time and life events can't tarnish.

I have another friend, Chris, whom I met while attending church. He's an accomplished architect and enjoys great notoriety in his field. We became friends and have had several lunches together, celebrated when his wife, Melody, became pregnant after many years of trying, praying and tears...I was there on their daughter's first birthday, and we try to get together whenever our busy schedules allow. We both would like to spend more time together, but we don't get together as much as we would like. While we have some wonderful shared experiences we haven't yet achieved the depth of relationship that we both desire. By comparison, we're relatively newer friends. And we have the hope of becoming lifelong friends.

My friendships with Ron and Chris are both cherished relationships. They are just different, that's all. Ron and I are the same age, went to the same schools and met when we were younger. Chris is several years younger than me, we met under different circumstances and our best years are ahead of us.

I'm also confident that there will be friends that I don't even know right now. We'll meet somehow and we'll find some common ground and our relationship will grow. But as of right now, we don't know each other.

Since this book is about fundraising, I'm pretty certain you can sense where I'm going here. In your ministry, you have faithful core donors who have given to your organization for years. These "old friends" stick with you year in and year out. You've likely met some of them and perhaps have gotten to know the names of their children, what they do for a living, and may have even spent some time in their homes. Like all close relationships, you've enjoyed the gift of time together.

Then one day, while you're reviewing your core donor giving, you realize that some of your core donors haven't given for a year or two. If you're like me, you might find yourself scratching your head and asking, "I wonder what's going on here? I sure hope we haven't offended them in some way." When I served in a ministry this was about the time I started asking our CEO or one of our major gift officers if they knew of any reason why these donors have "lapsed" in their giving. Most often I received an answer that left me with a knot in my stomach... "I don't have a clue..."

The queasiness in my innards came from the thought, "I wonder how many other core donors are becoming former core donors? And what can we do NOW to reinvigorate relationships with these special friends who are slipping further away? The good news is, there are things you can do to reactivate donors who have slowed or ceased in their giving. But there's even better news! Once reactivated, these precious friends of your ministry can and will become even more supportive!

This Rule #47, *Old friends are better than new friends or even no friends*...is a very encouraging one! It deserves a significant part of our attention and energy. But for some reason we tend to spend more of our resources acquiring new friends (donors) than we do in hanging on to the friends who've already proven their friendship over and over, through their faithful giving.

So...just how do we go about reactivating donors who've lapsed in their giving? It's really not that complicated. All we need to do is recognize that we have a problem and then use time-honored, effective strategies that experienced fundraisers have used for years.

We have more communication channels at our disposal than ever before. So let's use them! But let's also be careful here and use our resources wisely. The cheapest thing to do would be to send them an email saying, "We've missed you!" Since we're already swimming upstream here in trying to reverse a negative trend, we'd be wise to use the *more effective* strategies that will yield the highest number of reactivated donors rather than the cheapest approach.

Be careful reading further now because I'm about to encourage you to "go to the dark side" of fundraising (being a somewhat reputable fundraiser, I often find it necessary to give this advance warning because of the nature of what I'm about to recommend).

Telemarketing...there, I've said it! This communication channel has caused more nonprofit leaders to gasp, blink and then hold up their hand at arm's length, indicating the universal sign for HALT! This is quickly followed by, "WE DON'T DO TELEMARKETING! I HATE IT AND I WON'T IRRITATE MY DONORS WITH THIS INVASION OF THEIR PRIVACY! Besides, nobody has a landline anymore."

At this point, if I were a therapist, I would recommend to the CEO that she consider taking a few deep, cleansing breaths. But because I'm a fundraiser I just begin citing the stunning financial results that other ministries are experiencing, then quickly follow up with full assurance that ALL of the telemarketing phone callers are people of faith and carefully trained to not be pushy. About one third to one half of all CEOs end up agreeing to test this approach, and boy are they glad they did. Just as an example, one ministry reactivated 3,700 lapsed donors and realized a $3-to-$1 return on investment.

There's also comfort offered in the truth that if a calling campaign is not working, it can be paused, adjustments can be made, and then calling can resume. In the unlikely event that the campaign simply isn't working, it can be halted at any time.

It's probably prudent here to cite Rule #3 from *The Rules of Fundraising, Neither you or I get to make the rules.* It's a fact, there are rules to fundraising, and we don't get a vote as to what they are. We *can* choose to ignore them, but at our own peril; the peril of losing our core donors while at the same time paying a premium price to acquire new donors and cultivating them to the point where they become core donors.

Lastly, I would like to dip into my fundraising toolbox and offer a less contentious approach using all channels available to you (that allow for complete personalization). It was designed to *remind* "lapsed donors" that they are lapsed without producing shame or guilt. It's quite simple really, and it can be used with virtually any appeal for funds. It involves inserting a paragraph into your appeal that reads something like this:

"Your gift of $XX.XX in [Month] of [Year] really made a difference in helping to save and change lives. Would you consider making another gift of $XX.XX today?"

This simple reminder helps the donor realize that perhaps it's been a while since they've given. It might cause them to look through their check register to see if this information is accurate. Perhaps they thought their spouse was giving, and this will often yield another gift. The result is the renewing of an old friendship!

Another highly effective approach I recommend is to include all lapsed donors in traditional direct mail donor acquisition efforts. Both channels should be used since the results from phone calling do not significantly impact the success of the direct mail donor acquisition mailing.

As a reminder, the rule we are considering here, #47: *Old friends are better than new friends or even no friends...*

Note: a comprehensive discussion of acquiring new donors is found in Rule #23 of *The Rules of Fundraising,* page 149.

RULE #48
"Talk to your donors, not about yourself."

Quite frankly, I'm disappointed in myself that I haven't spoken to this rule before now. It's such a critical rule that I should have included it in my first book, *The Rules of Fundraising*.

I think the year was 1991. If you were alive and old enough to remember, you might have heard:

- George H.W. Bush was President of the United States.
- Brian Mulroney was the Prime Minister of Canada.
- Boris Yeltsin was the first freely elected President of Russia.
- The Soviet Union ceased to exist after the resignation of Mikhail Gorbachev.
- Kuwait was invaded by the Iraqi forces of Saddam Hussein.
- Allies launched Operation Desert Storm to repel Iraqi forces from Kuwait.
- Jeffrey Dahmer was arrested as a serial killer.
- Rodney King was beaten, on camera, in California.
- The Internet was made available for unrestricted commercial use.
- 1 million computers were using the Internet.

- Microsoft released MS DOS 5.0.
- Several memorable movies were released, e.g., *Thelma & Louise, Silence of the Lambs,* and *Father of the Bride.*
- Doug Shaw began employing the use of Donor-Focused Strategic Marketing™ on behalf of ministries.

Well...you probably didn't hear about this last one. But this was about the time when I first came to realize that donors would respond at a higher level when their direct mail letters began to speak TO them rather than ABOUT the ministry appealing to them.

What do I mean by this?

Imagine yourself going out to dinner with someone who spends the ENTIRE evening talking about herself. What's the likelihood that you will want to do this again anytime soon?

As one who has worked inside a ministry, I know the feeling of commitment it takes to live inside of a ministry community; I've experienced the passion for the mission of the organization and the deep desire to change and save lives. Of course, all of this requires funding in order to sustain and grow the organization.

I, too, gave into the temptation to tell as many people as possible ABOUT our ministry. I wanted EVERYONE to get involved. Little did I realize that I was behaving like that annoying TV commercial that gets played over and over while you're trying to watch your favorite program. The feeling comes close to hearing fingers scratching on a chalkboard (these are old slate boards attached to the walls where liquid writing surfaces or digital screens now hang).

But the good news is there is a way to cut through all the noise and involve donors and prospective donors in the ministry you serve.

Over time I began to identify two kinds of fundraising communication:

1. Institutionally focused communication and
2. Donor-focused communication

INSTITUTIONALLY FOCUSED ORGANIZATION

DONOR

ORGANIZATION

LIVES CHANGED

Institutionally focused communication places the emphasis on what YOUR MINISTRY is doing, e.g.:

This year The Heavenly Network has provided over 100,000 listeners on 900 stations with life-changing books and digital recordings, 1,000 people have made personal professions of faith, and tens of thousands have expressed how their lives have been changed through our broadcasts. Providing live streaming of our programs online has broadened The Heavenly Network's reach to over 50,000,000 people.

DONOR-FOCUSED ORGANIZATION

DONOR

ORGANIZATION

**LIVES
CHANGED**

<u>Donor-focused communication places the emphasis on what
God is doing through your donors, e.g.</u>:

*This year, the Lord has used your generous gifts to enable The
Heavenly Network to provide over 100,000 life-changing books
and digital recordings to our listeners!*

*In addition, through your giving, praying and volunteering,
we now air our programs on 900 stations! The Lord has used
your gifts to lead 1,000 women and men to make personal
professions of faith in Him, and tens of thousands have expressed
how their lives have been changed through broadcasts you've
made possible. Because you care and give, we are now able to
provide live streaming of all of our broadcasts to a listening
audience of over 50,000,000 people.*

You can see how the first approach doesn't *involve* the
donor, while the second not only involves the donor but is

more theologically correct in that it *gives the glory to God as He works through those who support this broadcast ministry.*

By employing the donor-focused approach to EVERY communication sent to donors and prospects, I've come to see much higher levels of engagement and response. You can do this too! A simple way to begin this approach is to write the way you are used to writing, and then sit back and ask yourself the question, "Now how can I write the donor *into* this communication?"

This is why Rule #48: *Talk to your donors, not about yourself* exists, to help generate greater levels of involvement from the donors who believe in your ministry. Happy writing!

NOTES:

RULE #49
"Response is better than admiration."

So it's that time again, when you find yourself sitting in front of your computer or perhaps you're in a meeting with several people on your development team. It's time to determine the strategies and tactics that you will employ to move your donors and prospects to give. If you're like me, it can be an extremely stressful time.

What often goes through my mind is the thought, "What I'm about to think, in my very own brain, is actually going to determine if this ministry is going to have the income it needs to fulfill its mission." Amazing, isn't it? It's all about *ideas*.

Growing up, I used to watch my dad build fireplaces, flagstone sidewalks and even entire buildings out of masonry. It was tangibility at its best. When he finished a job, he'd wash off his mason's trowel, clean up the job site and climb into his pickup. His work was solid, and when it was done, you could see it. Where once a grassy lot lay, somebody's house now stood. It was a place to shelter them, keep them safe, a place to raise their children, a place to celebrate the milestones of life.

But you and I live in the information age. What we think is what's important. What we think determines other people's actions. Concepts that originated in the depths of our brain cells become food for hungry people, faith for those in need of hope, Bibles for entire language groups, and medicine for the sick and dying.

For some, the thought of doing strategy causes you to open your snack drawer and start pumping Cheetos® into your mouth. For others, it's making the switch from Diet Coke® to Classic Coke®; nothing like caffeine and full-blown sugar to get the creative juices flowing.

But why would you feel angst? After all, developing strategies and tactics should be a time of excitement, a time of free-flowing ideas and brainstorming. This is when your creativity gets to shine! This is when you may be tempted to say, "Look, Ma, I designed that great-looking newsletter!"

Journeymen fundraisers know that to approach this critical time with a spirit of assumptions and subjectivity is a walk amongst the gravestones of former development officers. Whew! Are you feeling the angst yet?

The veterans of philanthropy know that a fundraiser's ideas must be grounded in the responses they deliver. In other words, do your ideas actually deliver the results you expect? As expert fundraiser Billy Vaudry says, "Creativity judges us!" It's a great way of saying creativity is only effective if it generates the response we need.

This rule: #49: *Response is better than admiration,* exists because there is so very much depending on it.

Knowing this rule and the other rules of fundraising is absolutely essential when developing strategies and tactics that work. Perhaps a helpful tool for you to use when engaged in this critical time of idea creation is to think of *admiration* as a "like" on social media; it feels nice or even great (if your volume is high), but generating *responses* (read: gifts) is what you need to accomplish your mission.

NOTES:

RULE #50
"Dance with the one that brung ya."

I think it was sometime in my sophomore year at Renton High School that I was asked to go to "The Tolo" by my friend Annie. I've heard other names for this kind of dance, like "Turnabout" or "Sadie Hawkins." I don't know if kids still do this today, but it was the one time of year when a high school girl could ask a high school boy to a dance. And I couldn't believe it when Annie asked ME!

Renton, or RHS, as we called it, was a 3,000-student, semi-urban high school on the south side of Seattle. The student body had grown so large by 1967 that we had three different lunch hours. So Annie and I would sit with a couple of other people and try to survive the raucous event known as lunch.

This period would usually start quite normally: we'd line up and grab an aluminum tray with several large dimples in it to keep the juices from our canned peaches from running into our Salisbury steak. As we made our way past the "serving ladies," who stared us down as they pounded the day's scrumptious fare into our tray with such force it required a firm grip, I couldn't help noticing that all of the ladies wore the same kind of hairnet and smock apron. At the time I didn't realize their garb was worn to protect US from THEM.

I thought it was to protect THEM from the noxious globs of protein they were slamming onto our trays.

Emerging from this grumbling line of students, having paid my $1.25, the ritual of finding my group began. The lunchroom was quite large and filled with heavy-duty picnic-style metal tables. With 1,000 students in each lunch period, it took a few seconds to locate my preferred tablemates. Usually somebody from our group would watch so when we paid and turned to survey the room, they would wave furiously until we saw them and threaded our way through the tables of slurping students to finally squeeze into a place being saved for us. Annie was often the one who had saved a seat for me.

Once seated, the entire ordeal left us with about seven minutes to actually eat what hadn't slid off our tray in transit.

Several times I remember how suddenly the jam-packed room became strangely quiet. When this occurred we all waited with an almost ecstatic sense of anticipation. It usually started with something as small as a pickle or a piece of carrot thrown expertly across several tables into the face of one of the student diners. We all knew the next move. A rowdy upperclassman would jump up and yell, "FOOD FIGHT!"

Eruption is the only word I can apply to the scene as it played out. In less than 10 seconds the entire room would stand and throw, fling, lob or otherwise launch the entire contents of their trays across the ducking and diving bodies of young women and men. The air was filled with food shrapnel flying and clinging globs of reconstituted mashed potatoes that hit and slid down the sides of panic-stricken faces. The floor became so slippery with spilled drinks and mushed up food that standing was not an option. So we all dove under our tables with the hope that we could make it to the McDonald's across the street before the class bell rang. It was here, under the table, that Annie asked me to the Tolo.

Now to a 15-year-old boy, being asked to a dance by a girl of Annie's caliber was life-changing. She was a pretty girl who was very comfortable in her own skin. We were never an "item," if you will, but when you eat lunch with someone several times a week, adolescent attraction is always a possibility.

I think I must have rushed home that afternoon and checked in the mirror to see if I had grown some whiskers. Why else would she have chosen me?

The Friday before the Tolo I was in the hallway, making my way to my next class, when Tom, one of my best friends, came alongside and said, "I hear you're going to Tolo with Annie." Ah, so word was getting out! I loved it. People were talking about my good fortune. I could feel myself straightening up just a bit as I replied casually, "Yeah, no big deal." Then Tom said something that turned my world upside down. "She's been dating Maury, you know, but I hear she broke up with him."

My head began spinning as I moved on to my next class. I don't even remember sitting down at my desk or anything the teacher had to say. I didn't even know that Annie was dating anybody, let alone Maury. He was the tallest, most muscular football star at RHS! I was a D-E-A-D man! How was I supposed to dance with Annie knowing Maury was in the same room, probably plotting to "take me out" in the parking lot afterwards?!

I don't even remember how I arrived at the Tolo. Did

Annie pick me up? Did I just meet her there? All I know is when I saw her she looked lovely. For an infinitesimal moment my excitement returned. We stood there talking when the band began playing a Buffalo Springfield song, "Hey, what's that sound? Everybody look what's going down." Annie said, "Wanna dance?"

I'm an absolute mess. Here I am dancing with a cute girl, who had invited ME, and I'm fearing a head blow that will send me flying spread-eagle across the dance floor, but Annie didn't appear concerned at all. So we danced.

When the band took a break, Annie excused herself, and I thought she was going to the restroom. But instead she walked casually up to Maury, who was with another girl. They chatted briefly, and then she turned and came back to ME! That was it? No killer stare from Maury, no explanation from Annie, she just simply came back to dance with her date. I was at a loss, so I simply danced with the one who invited me.

Whenever I hear the phrase, "Dance with the one that brung ya," my mind returns to that fateful adolescent evening. For our purposes today, this phrase, or rule, if you will, means something entirely different to me.

Rule #50: *Dance with the One That Brung Ya,* reminds me to *not abandon the fundraising strategies and tactics that produce the greatest amount of return for the ministries I serve.*

According to a recent Data and Marketing Association presentation by Blackbaud, at this point in time, 7.1% of all giving in the U.S. is generated from online sources. Whenever I'm speaking to development officers, they seem surprised by how low this figure is compared to the 92.9% that continues to

<u>be generated through offline sources</u> (these numbers are very similar in Canada).

About 10 years ago, online represented about 1% of all giving in the U.S. So we're obviously seeing significant growth in this area. Mark Loux, a colleague and third generation fundraiser, believes online revenue will continue to grow at this pace until we see about 35% from online efforts. He's predicting that at that time a "tipping point" will occur and online will become a significantly higher source of gift revenue.

As I understand our craft, we all need to be using ALL channels that can contribute income to our ministry. Here at Douglas Shaw & Associates, we have invested heavily in digital services. We are currently providing digital strategy, execution and reporting for nonprofit organizations in three countries on two continents. We fully expect digital revenue to continue to become a major force in direct response fundraising.

The attractiveness of digital fundraising is growing due to its low cost compared with offline strategies. But there are other reasons for being proactive in digital communications.

There's a lesson we can learn from all the catalogs you and I receive in our mailboxes. It seems like there is a catalog for everything, every stage of life and every interest. It may help us a bit to think through our own personal actions when a catalog arrives at our home. Here's what happens at my house:

1. We retrieve the catalogs from our mailbox (fall is a BIG season for this).
2. We quickly sort through them to determine which ones we want to look through.
3. We toss the rest.

4. If the catalog we keep is presenting something we need or want NOW we may even look at it right then at the kitchen counter.

5. If the catalog is from a company we've purchased from before but not offering something we need or want right now, we may keep it for a later look (usually we just end up tossing it).

6. For the catalog offering something we need or want right now, we will discuss it and likely do what?

We open our laptop and go online to see if we can get it cheaper through Amazon (who often delivers it for free), or we order directly from the company who sent the catalog.

This is what many donors do too! When you send them a direct mail appeal, several of them will open their laptop and (if your website is up to date AND easy to navigate) they will make their gift online.

Catalog companies scaled back their printed catalogs once they realized they could create online versions. At first it felt like a real cost savings! But sales immediately declined. What did they learn? *Printed catalogs drive people to their website.*

The same is true for direct mail appeals and ministry newsletters! There are some donors who have overcome their distrust of giving online and prefer to use this channel. This is why we are wise to provide digital options for ALL offline direct response fundraising efforts.

The whole reason for my tale of Annie and the dance was to illustrate, in story form, Rule #50. As people, we tend to remember principles or rules better if told as a story. Hopefully it will serve you in your own journey to embrace these two truths:

1. *"Dance with the one that brung ya"* is a rule and therefore must be followed, lest we abandon the proven direct response channels that have brought us to where we are today, i.e., 92.9% of all giving in the U.S. comes from offline sources, AND

2. Online presence is not an option; it HAS to be available. While 7.1% of all giving in the U.S. is online, much of the online giving is *driven there from offline sources like direct mail and newsletters.*

NOTES:

RULE #51
"Small donors can cost you money."

Seasoned fundraising professionals are not as easily impressed as they were when they first began their journey on the path of philanthropic encouragement. What used to please them, like acquiring a lot of new donors, now leaves them asking the question, "Did we acquire the right kind of new donors?"

How can ANY donor be less than the "right kind"?

Let's take a different look at what has become known as *The Widow's Mite:*

While teaching in the temple, Jesus is addressing the crowd gathered around Him. Some are asking questions to learn from Him; others are attempting to trap Him with His own words. Jesus knows what the deal is. He begins offering up wisdom that none can dispute. After a few rounds with the Pharisees and Herodians, He warns those listening to Him,

"Beware of the scribes, who like to walk around in long robes, love greetings in the market places, the best seats in the synagogues, and the best places at feasts, who devour widows' houses, and for a pretense long prayers. These will receive greater condemnation."
(Luke 20: 45-47)

It's then that He decides to move over near the treasury. He takes a seat and watches as the multitude are putting money into the treasury. There are some high rollers today, putting in large amounts of money.

Among the crowd is a poor widow. She drops in two small copper coins. He calls His disciples to Him and provides them with a perspective quite out of step with what they have just seen.

> *"Truly I say to you that this poor widow has put in more than all; for all these out of their abundance have put in offerings for God, but she out of her poverty put in all the livelihood that she had."* (Luke 21: 3-4)

As a person of faith and a fundraising consultant, this kind of wisdom rocks my world! It speaks to my thirsty soul by providing the living water that only Jesus can give. The Son of God has linked the giving of money to the *motive* in the giver's heart. What human being can dispute the value of what we now call, "The Widow's Mite"? No one.

As a ministry leader you too witness sacrificial giving, and it touches you deeply. As it most certainly should! EVERY gift is to be cherished as God's provision through His people.

And to be clear, we must thank EVERY donor for EVERY gift. An appropriate thank-you letter should be snail mailed (via 1st-class postage) to every person who supports your ministry regardless of gift size (again, our standard is within 24-48 hours).

So, how in the world *can* a "Widow's Mite" hurt your ministry?

It usually occurs when we seek to acquire new donors for ministry. When very small gifts are solicited, say gifts under $15.00, donors will respond with small gifts, because, you may remember, people generally give what they are asked to give!

There's a problem with asking for small initial gifts. **Those who give them very seldom give larger gifts.** It can and usually does result in a ministry acquiring a significant number of small initial gifts. This may mean more donors are acquired, but *these donors will not upgrade, leaving the ministry with donors who will cost the ministry more than the gifts they give.*

We can and must make sound stewardship decisions. While it's true and biblical that ALL gifts should be appreciated and acknowledged, *it is essential to your ministry's health and growth that larger gifts be solicited during donor acquisition.* Our experience indicates that new donors giving gifts larger than $15.00 are much more likely to upgrade their giving in the days and months ahead.

It's worth mentioning here that every ministry will receive small gifts. In addition to honoring these donations with a thank-you letter, just as you would larger gifts, you will want to limit the number of appeals to donors who fall into this category. If your larger donors receive 12-15 appeals for funds annually, this group should be limited to 4-5 of your most popular appeals. This will give them the opportunity to become larger donors.

So, I encourage you to graciously receive and honor the widow's mite, but to not seek them in your donor acquisition! As this rule states, *"Small donors can cost you money!"*

NOTES:

RULE #52
"The true value of a donor is seen over time."

I can remember the board meeting as if it were happening today. The memory and principle has stayed with me even though what I witnessed occurred in 1991.

All of the board and senior staff of a large East Coast rescue mission were seated at a long table down in the bowels of this 100-year-old building. I had just presented a plan for this vital ministry that recommended spending $250,000 for 1 million pieces of direct mail donor acquisition. It was projected to be a break-even proposition that would acquire 10,000 new donors.

The ministry CEO knew it would require board approval for an expenditure of this size. He also knew he could not adequately explain the true value of this significant step toward the growth of the ministry. He invited me, and one of the owners of the firm I worked for, to attend and answer any questions the board may have.

Most of the board members were highly successful businessmen. They were used to investing principles, and yet, when it came to the rescue mission, they were very wary of spending donor dollars on a break-even effort. It was their general consensus that donors to this cause would object should they hear of this effort.

As experienced as they were in business, they had little knowledge, if any, of how donor acquisition worked and why it is a necessity for every ministry to maintain and grow.

One of the board members asked, "Can't we just spend enough to produce a reasonable profit? Maybe $100,000?"

The concept of acquiring donors who would create value over time was not easily understood by business people, who were used to producing immediate profits for their shareholders.

In addition, they were exhibiting behavior that many journeymen fundraisers have observed over their years of service. There's a bit of a phenomenon that can be detected in some board members. Many of them are invited onto boards because of their business acumen, but a strange thing happens when they set foot inside the nonprofit boardroom... *they check their business sense at the door!*

Those of us who have witnessed this trend have developed a theory about this phenomenon. Our prevailing theory, at the moment, is that once board members step out of their offices and into the ministry, they assume the posture of experts rather than learners.

So, our job that day was to become teachers to experts!

My employer was standing at the head of the table addressing the group. He began by asking the question, "Does anyone here have a dollar?" The board members looked around the table and one of them responded, "Yes," pulling a single dollar bill from his pocket.

My employer reached into his own pocket and retrieved a

twenty-dollar bill. "Would you like to trade?" he asked.

"Absolutely!" replied the board member.

So the trade was made, and a small chuckle worked its way around the table. My employer certainly had their attention now.

Then my employer said, "Do you have another dollar?"

Several board members responded, "I do!"

But my employer remained focused on the man he had just traded with. "Would you like to trade another dollar again?"

"All day," the board member said enthusiastically.

So another exchange occurred, one dollar for another twenty-dollar bill.

Then came the clincher!

My employer said, "Would you like the ministry to make this same trade 250,000 times?" Questions poured forth about how this could be possible. It was such a simple illustration, yet powerful. The board began assuming the posture of learners.

They learned that spending $250,000 today would not only net the ministry 10,000 donors but also, with the new donor's giving frequency increasing and donation amount growing, the ministry would net $5,000,000 over the next five years. And the good news was, they could repeat this donor acquisition effort every year!

The budget was approved...unanimously!

This is why Rule #52: *The true value of a donor is seen over time,* exists!

NOTES:

RULE #53
"Listening to donors is often talked about but seldom done."

The picnic table was old and weathered gray with light green stripes of moss on its legs where it met the lawn. It was where my dad would sit in his overalls covered by a heavy flannel shirt, with his cap angled slightly on his head, and drink his coffee.

When I went to visit my folks, often I would end up out at this table with my dad. On one of my visits, my dad's oldest brother, Uncle Bob, was visiting too, and the two retired bricklayers sat there, talking and smoking their unfiltered cigarettes.

I had been sitting quietly listening to the family lore being exchanged between them. "Now Joe, he works for a living," my dad was saying to Bob. I thought for a second and then realized what had just been said, so I spoke up, "So you think I don't work for a living?" The look that transpired between the two bricklayers was priceless.

In my dad's world, men who worked with their hands were said to "work for a living." People who worked in offices were often referred to as "paper pushers." They had become so engrossed in their conversation that they had completely forgotten that I was there. I had caught them in the act of totally being themselves.

I also realized that through my many years of going to school and now working as a fundraising consultant, I had crossed the great cultural chasm of class. They were "working class" and I was a "paper pusher," or in more sophisticated terms, "white collar middle class."

It felt strange to realize that I had traveled so far from my roots. I felt a bit like a voyeur, watching this shared bond between two men who knew the backbreaking world of sweat, calloused hands and hourly wages.

About a year later I experienced a similar feeling of voyeurism, but it was a completely different set of circumstances. I was sitting behind a two-way mirrored glass wall observing donors who were talking about their giving experiences involving a ministry that I represented.

We were conducting focus groups for a ministry that wanted to know how they were being perceived by some of their current supporters and past supporters. I was sitting behind the glass with the ministry's CEO. It didn't occur to me just how difficult the process would be for him until he said, "I feel like I'm watching heart surgery...being conducted on me!"

The whole experience was quite fascinating! The participants were all told by the moderator that there were observers behind the glass. They each made a sidelong glance at the mirror but soon forgot that we were even there.

The information gleaned from these sessions was immensely helpful in learning the perceptions of people who gave to this ministry and to other causes as well. Some of the questions we had the moderator ask were:

- How long have you supported this ministry?
- How often do you give?
- What prompted you to begin giving?
- Do you believe your gifts are used well?
- What do you like best about this ministry?
- What do you least like about this ministry?
- If you could change anything about how the ministry communicates with you, what would it be?
- If you could say anything to the leadership of this ministry, what would it be?
- Would you recommend that your friends support this ministry?
- Other than giving donations, are there other ways you would like to be involved?
- Would you be willing to tell us how many other organizations you support?
- Would you be willing to tell us what other organizations you support?

During each of the four focus groups, the moderator would excuse himself and come back to us in our seats behind the mirror and ask, "Are there any other questions you would like for me to ask this group?" Sometimes we had additional questions from something that was said by the participants, but most often we did not.

We noticed two additional trends that were quite interesting during these groups:

1. When the donors were asked "How often do you give?" many of the respondents indicated they gave more often than our giving histories indicated. We knew this

because we had all their gift transactions in front of us during the focus groups.

2. Lapsed donors indicated that they were still active in their support, even though their last recorded gift was over 24 months ago!

All of the incredibly helpful insights were noted and then used to form the basis of a much larger telephone survey of a statistically valid sampling of the remainder of the donor file. In all we received VERY helpful insights to help us modify our communication with both donors and lapsed donors.

Focus groups fall into a category commonly referred to as *qualitative* research. The broader survey, by telephone, was considered *quantitative research*. Both types of research were conducted to give us the most accurate information.

The groups provided us with not only verbal responses but body language as well (about 65% of all communication is through body language).

The phone survey provided statistical validation of what we had learned from the groups. Together, this approach provided us with information to help us dramatically increase both gift size and frequency from active donors.

The lapsed donor insights increased our ability to reactivate donors who had not given for some time.

This Rule, #53: *Listening to donors is often talked about but seldom done,* exists to help us generate increased income from our active and lapsed donors.

Many ministries view "research" as a luxury they cannot afford. Experienced fundraisers know this is not the case. Those who have long traveled the roads of philanthropy understand the high value of research and enjoy increased income that far exceeds the cost of the research. It pays, literally, to listen to your donors.

NOTES:

MORE RULES OF FUNDRAISING

RULE #54
"It's OK to not have all the answers."

Much of my early life was spent on farms and ranches in the Midwest and in the West. To a kid, growing up in these earthy environments I was able to meet some VERY interesting characters, like Clarence.

He lived on a dry farm across the road from my family in the mountains of Washington State. A "dry farm" is totally dependent upon nature to provide the moisture needed to grow wheat and hay. Most highly productive farms that we often see along our nation's interstates are irrigated by large aluminum pipe systems that use huge sprinklers to grow alfalfa and soybeans. But where we lived, people couldn't afford such extravagances.

I often found myself sitting with Clarence around lunchtime drinking instant coffee and listening to the small portable radio with its antenna up, sitting on Clarence's metal TV tray. Paul Harvey provided the news as only he could do it. His squeaky voice delivered the news with personal insights and plenty of homey humor. The mere sound of his voice warmed us like a good fire.

Clarence and I would often talk about high school basketball. "Do you think Oroville will beat Tonasket this year?" Clarence would ask. "Hope so," I would respond. "We've got a pretty good team this year."

Sitting there with Clarence, I learned much about this man who spent his days and nights tending to his dusty crops and small herd of cattle. He would sit there in his dirty, sweat-stained long underwear and worn-out jeans, and tell tales about the mountains of snow in the "winter of '49," or the summer when there was no rain to be found.

As all kids do, I asked Clarence a lot of questions about farming, and sometimes I would venture into his personal life, which was quite a mystery to me. I knew he had been married once but, "It hadn't worked out." I never asked why. He didn't have any children that I knew of. Most of his life was centered on his 500 acres spanning this high mountain valley we both called home.

I greatly enjoyed my lunches with Clarence. He was easy to talk to, and he didn't use big words that kids wouldn't understand. I thought perhaps he didn't know any fancy words, so you can imagine my surprise the day he revealed that he had graduated from both high school and college!

Another fact he surprised me with was how he spent the winter. Every year, late in the fall, he would staple big sheets of plastic all around the walls inside his living room, bathroom and kitchen. It sealed the house and even covered his stairway leading to the upstairs. In the winter, the couch was his only bed. The small brick fireplace supplied all the heat he needed. When I asked why he did this, he replied, "Takes less firewood."

And when I asked Clarence a question that he didn't know the answer to, he simply replied, "I don't know."

When Clarence didn't know something, it didn't frustrate me. It just caused me to trust him all the more. Here was a man who lived his life as he saw fit. He didn't seem to worry about what others thought of him. If you asked him a question he would answer it as best he could. If he didn't know something he simply said so.

Fundraisers who have been around the barn a few times know the value in admitting what we know and what we don't know. It sounds like pretty simple stuff, but if it were, I think I would be better at practicing this earthy wisdom. To this day I still find myself pausing when someone asks me something about fundraising that I have yet to learn. It requires all of the character I can muster to simply say, "I don't know." I am a fundraising consultant, after all. I make my living by knowing stuff that others want and need to know. I hope that, on a good day, I can do Clarence proud.

The valuable aspect of knowing what we don't know is the curiosity it creates in someone who wants to have a life of learning. Albert Einstein once said, "It is a miracle that curiosity survives formal education."

Rule #54 says, *It's OK to NOT have all the answers,* and when we admit this to ourselves and to others, they respect us all the more. It also builds trust when you *do* know something. Why? I don't know.

NOTES:

RULE #55
"Ineffective board members can do great harm to a ministry."

I remember my first board meeting for one of the larger ministries I served many years ago. I was working for another consulting firm back then as Vice President for Client Services. Part of my position required that I work with all levels of leadership within the ministry I served.

Being a little intimidated and nervous to be in the presence of this important body of leaders, I made certain that I was very well prepared to answer any questions they might ask of me.

I arrived early, out of respect, and did not take a seat, but rather deferred until I knew where everyone else was going to sit and then inquired where they would like me to be.

I watched with curiosity as the various members arrived. A few came early, but most kind of trickled in over the course of about 20 minutes. Upon entering the boardroom most of them greeted each other, shook hands with me and then began to make small talk until the board chair finally arrived, about 10 minutes late.

While we were waiting for the board chair, one of the members sat down and leaned back in his chair. Another member commented to me, "Look out for Charlie over there," nodding to the man leaning back in his chair. "He's so cheap he still owns his first comb." Sure enough, as if on cue, Charlie produced a small black comb from his pants pocket and held it up for examination. "He's right! Here it is! I've had this comb for over 20 years, and it still works like new." I must have appeared a little shocked as I looked at Charlie's comb. It was filthy with stuff I did NOT want to inquire about, and it was missing about five teeth!

My feelings of intimidation began melting away and were quickly replaced by concern. "Is this person going to be making decisions about the future of this ministry?" I thought to myself. I just gave a wan smile and hoped the others yet to arrive had more to offer. My mind went to a quote from fundraising great Jerry Panas, who has often written, "You get the board you deserve."

As it turned out, there were several other members who entered the room shortly thereafter who were well-dressed and kept their combs in their pockets. Seats were chosen and notepads were pulled from briefcases in preparation for our meeting.

Once everyone was gathered, and the board chair had arrived with the CEO, the meeting was quickly called to order. I had been briefed that I would be first on the agenda, and once my portion was complete, I should excuse myself so they could finish their work in private.

After a quick greeting, the board chair opened the meeting in prayer and turned to another member who had been assigned to provide a short devotional. I don't remember too much about his message, just that it wasn't short, and it was unclear how the subject related to either the ministry or its mission.

When I was asked to formally introduce myself and the company I represented, I proceeded as directed. This led into the question at hand, "Could the ministry generate more income to meet the growing needs of the community?"

Several basic questions followed my presentation, which I appeared to answer to their satisfaction. I was thanked, and I packed up my things and made my exit.

The next morning, I had breakfast with the CEO. He informed me that the board had indeed been satisfied with my presentation, and they were looking forward to seeing the ministry's income increase to meet the growing needs.

After several minutes of discussion, the CEO leaned toward me in the restaurant and said quietly, "We really need to move some of these people off the board." I felt relief begin to flow through my shoulders as I sat back in my chair. It was good to know that the CEO was seeing the reality of the situation.

Having heard his comment, I felt the freedom to express my concern about Charlie. "Oh," the CEO said, "He's just one of about six guys that need to go. But it's going to take some time. Some of these people have been on the board for over 30 years!"

Time was one thing the ministry did not have. The city was threatening to move the ministry to get the unsightly building out of view. If ever the ministry needed the strength of visionary leadership, it was now.

I have actually removed myself from any board commitments since realizing I don't have the time to give ministries what they need from me as a board member. I believe I serve them best as a fundraising consultant.

Selecting board members should be one of the most

important duties of the board and CEO. A formal position description is an essential document to guide a board's nominating committee, as well as in setting expectations for candidates. It should be difficult to be selected to serve on a board. A ministry's reputation will determine much of the quality of board members it attracts. This is true for any sized ministry.

The dangers of allowing ineffective board members to serve are many:

- Their presence communicates who the ministry really is to its community and constituents.
- Voting or making decisions without proper knowledge can seriously diminish an organization's ability to accomplish its mission.
- Having board members who are "warming a chair" can prevent truly passionate and engaged people from considering service.
- Donors are expecting more and more from the charities they support; a strong, proactive board of trustees is an essential element in how much funding a major donor will commit to a ministry.

If any of this sounds familiar, then you know the truth of Rule #55: *Ineffective board members can do great harm to a ministry.*

RULE #56
"Effective board members are a precious gift to a ministry."

I love to hear a CEO or development officer say, "We have a great board!" This prized group of women and men provide many important functions, but their presence also contributes to an inspirational culture and spiritually vital environment for the entire ministry.

Over the past 35 years, I've had the privilege of being included in many board meetings and board retreats for numerous organizations. Most of them have been delightful experiences. Those times have served to remind me that highly functioning boards are indeed a precious gift to any ministry. One of my most memorable board meetings served as a showcase for what boards and ministries might aspire:

My portion of this meeting was, as is often the case, to make the case for spending more money to dramatically grow the donated income in order to prepare for future growth.

The CEO and Vice President of Development had very clear goals for the outcome of this meeting. They had taken the time to prepare the board development committee for the topic at hand, and the board chair was fully briefed and in agreement with what I was being asked to present.

The meeting was held during the lunch hour, and a buffet

lunch had been prepared for the members. The chair had arrived early and provided insights into the group dynamics of the board. I was forewarned that there would be some opposition, especially from one board member in particular. He was described as being VERY fiscally conservative, and to NOT expect him to appear pleased with ANY expenditure of money. The chair encouraged me to not be put off or discouraged by this. He further indicated that he, himself, would guide the discussion.

As the board members arrived, it was evident that most of them knew each other quite well and were at ease as they circulated amongst the group forming up in the line to fill their plates. I had been asked to join them for the lunch portion, and then the chair would introduce me and I would have precisely 20 minutes to present, with another 10 minutes for questions. Once my portion was completed, I was expected to make a speedy departure in order to maximize the time for the board to discuss and make decisions.

Because it was a large board, numbering about 24 members, I had brought a colleague along to manage my PowerPoint presentation so I could focus on the board's response rather than operating the PowerPoint presentation.

As foreseen, the prickly board member began shifting in his chair, and once the Q&A began he came out shooting. As promised, the chair maintained control of the meeting, allocating time for Mr. Prickly while allowing for several other members to speak as well.

It was truly a board meeting. The CEO was in attendance, but he did not attempt to run the meeting or respond to any board member questions or comments; he participated only as directed by the chair. It was also very clear that the board chair had the CEO's back.

I marveled at the ability of the chair to convene such a well-prepared and properly conducted meeting of very accomplished people from the community who had been carefully selected to sit on this board.

It was interesting for me to watch the dynamic of the board. Each member seemed to be aware that they were part of a prestigious team. It was known throughout this great city that to be invited to serve on this board was a compliment. Even Mr. Prickly seemed to know that his opinion was in the minority and chose not to try to usurp the authority of the chair.

The board member questions ran longer than the allotted 10 minutes, but only because the chair knew it was time well spent and the issue at hand deserved the time expended. Finally, noting the time, the chair excused me and my colleague so the board could deliberate in private.

A few weeks later, while attending an annual ministry event, the board chair approached me and gave me a compliment I will always cherish: "Doug, you help us to stand tall!" I'm moved again as I write this, because I know my contribution was only possible because this ministry had chosen its board chair and board VERY carefully. This effective board was clearly a gift to this ministry!

NOTES:

RULE #57
"An ineffective CEO will cause great harm to your ministry."

He was a very odd man. Some called him quirky; others just called him strange. He had an almost addictive relationship with any new executive technology that entered the marketplace. The latest phone, watch, radio or electronic dictating equipment claimed his attention immediately. He had them purchased and reveled in showing them to anyone who entered his office. It was almost as if he needed these gadgets to assure himself that he was on the cutting edge of being what he interpreted as a CEO.

He was often heard making unnerving statements like:
- "Being a CEO would be great if it weren't for having to deal with people."
- "I've always wanted to be a millionaire, and now I control millions of dollars."

He was also a person who spent most of his time out of the office. When he wasn't travelling to some far off country, flying VIP status and staying in five-star hotels, he was usually found in his "study" at home. People who needed a meeting with him found themselves schlepping stacks of files to his house.

When he did make an appearance at work, he remained in his office that was vigilantly guarded by an executive assistant whom he required to refer to him as "Doctor So and So." This contributed greatly to what his leadership team referred to as the "Oval Office mentality" that he created and appeared to cherish.

In addition to the personality and cultural concerns I've described, there were many issues with decision-making. The "Doctor" avoided making decisions until often circumstances dictated that they were made for him. And the decisions he did get around to making were of significant magnitude and often not in the best interests of the organization. Unfortunately, the board of trustees allowed him to operate in this fashion for over a decade. In the end, he experienced a very messy departure with the ministry left in debt and experiencing significant turnover of highly talented employees.

Until I became a CEO myself (over 21 years ago), I didn't fully realize the many forces that come to bear on this critical position. Every single day there are issues that surface and decisions to be made that impact the entire organization, perhaps even the community, state, country, world and Kingdom!

To have an *ineffective leader* hold the position of CEO is a very serious setback to any ministry. To put it bluntly, people suffer when leadership fails them. Followers are often left without hope, direction and effectiveness in their own positions. In my experience, this critical leadership role must be safeguarded at all costs.

So, what are some of the telltale signs of an ineffective CEO? In reading the list below, I have seldom seen a CEO exhibit ALL of these shortcomings. No leader is perfect (believe me, I know this from continuing to learn more of my own limitations). But if a CEO has more than three or four of these deficits, people and ministries will suffer:

1. The inability to identify and communicate reality: Why does the ministry exist? Is it accomplishing its primary reasons for existence? What is the state of the health of the ministry? What works? What needs fixing? What should be abandoned? Are the followers of the CEO resourced to accomplish what is required of them? Do donors value and support the ministry at acceptable levels?

2. Indecision: Are the problems and opportunities of the ministry being grasped and acted upon in a timely manner? Does the CEO always seem to need more input prior to making decisions?

3. Conflict aversion: When conflicts arise (and they certainly will) both within and outside the ministry, are they acknowledged and resolved in a manner and timeframe that contributes to the health and vitality of the ministry? Or are there chronic issues or undercurrents holding the ministry back?

4. The inability to convene: Is a safe, orderly and productive environment created for the respectful discussion of issues and ideas? Or do most meetings feel like lectures?

5. Lack of clarity: Do all followers know what is expected of them? Do they know their responsibilities and are they empowered with the authority to carry them out? Are your requests for clarity dealt with in a reasonable amount of time?

6. <u>Lack of vigilance</u>: Is the overall health of the ministry being cared for? Is ministry relevance cherished and nurtured? Are problems and opportunities identified and prepared for in time to allow for a proactive stance? Are problems passively left until they resolve themselves to the detriment of the ministry?

7. <u>Inability to be curious</u>: Are directives the order of the day, or are questions and listening valued? Is continual learning practiced and encouraged? Does it feel like new ideas are discouraged?

8. <u>Low self-awareness</u>: Is there a pattern of awkward or socially inappropriate behavior that prohibits conventional conversation, breaking of trust, embarrassment or loss of hope?

9. <u>Struggles with proper boundaries</u>: Is emotional disrobing a frequent occurrence? Are invasive or immature behaviors keeping you from trusting leadership?

10. <u>Little interest in pursuing excellence</u>: Tradition and precedence seem to trump new ideas that could lead to corporate improvement?

11. <u>Limited ability to cast a vision for the ministry</u>: Is it difficult to be a follower because it's not clear where the organization is heading?

12. <u>Allowing the absence of, or unpredictable adherence to the ministry's core values</u>: Does the knowledge of what the ministry values in the way of appropriate behavior, culture and ultimate outcomes seem lacking? Are the expressed core values administered with continuing inconsistency?

13. <u>Values personal loyalty over competence and corporate health</u>: Is there a culture of "us and them" that pervades the organization? Is uncertainty of where you stand with the CEO the rule of the day?

14. <u>Appears to care more about the mission of the ministry than the donors who fund it</u>: Donors are seen and treated as though they are a means to an end rather than a key partner in ministry. Fundraising is tolerated as a "necessary evil" rather than a critical aspect of the ministry itself.

15. <u>Self-absorption</u>: Isolation and personal prestige, obsession with self-promotion and personal comfort define the leader. The "lifting up" of others appears to threaten the CEO.

Able followership requires able leadership. Rule #57: *An Ineffective CEO Will Cause Great Harm to Your Ministry,* is more prevalent when board members are disconnected from the corporate culture. While, in my eyes, *policy* boards are more helpful to ministries than *administrative* boards, it is *always* appropriate for boards to monitor the overall health of the organizations they serve. **Only they can provide the corrective action needed to protect those who carry out the mission of the ministry.**

NOTES:

RULE #58
"An effective CEO contributes to all that is good."

When I first met him I could see the intelligence in his eyes, which were focused upon me, taking my measure. He sat there in his chair with a calm demeanor. His hands were folded in his lap. Despite his calm exterior I could sense his intensity. This was clearly a man on a mission and in a hurry to accomplish it.

His leadership team surrounded the table where we were meeting. By scanning the room, I could see they were not only listening carefully, but they were also studying his demeanor as he spoke about his commitment to their cause. I could see they were totally in step with him in this great enterprise in which they were engaged.

I could tell he was serious when he said, "The quickest way to get fired as our agency would be for you to go around my team to get to me." This conversation took place nearly 10 years ago, but I still feel the earnestness of his statement. He didn't deliver this as a threat but as a firm boundary. I also remember the feeling of confidence and pride that his team exhibited at that moment. I couldn't help but believe him, and in my heart of hearts I wanted to be like him.

There was vulnerability in him too. He spoke openly about

how he had been fired from his previous position at another organization. The pain was still visible, but it was tempered by the great opportunity it afforded him to become CEO of this ministry. I never had the sense that he had failed in his previous job; he was just too big for it. This observation wasn't due to his words but rather the confident way he held himself, his convictions and the clarity exhibited in describing their mission.

More than a decade has passed since that first meeting, and my initial observations have been confirmed over and over. My company was hired to help them change the world, and it's clearly happening!

If I revealed his name, you wouldn't know it. That's not what he's about. He's totally focused on the calling he lives out and the innovation necessary to accomplish the vital mission he leads.

I've attended a few major donor weekends hosted by this ministry and have heard him say to those in attendance, "When we receive a request for funding, we are going to say 'Yes' until we can't say 'Yes' anymore!" By every indication, he and the ministry he leads have kept this commitment and gone far beyond where they were when I first heard these words.

He's never sought controversy, but he's led the ministry through many times of trial and come out the other side with innovative strides that have totally revolutionized the speed at which they are accomplishing their mission. And I still want to be like him...

This kind of leadership sounds like a tall order, doesn't it? Well...it is! Just think of the positive attributes that such an effective CEO gives to all who are impacted by their presence:

- You (as the fundraiser)
- Your colleagues
- Your donors
- Your industry
- Your ministry
- Your community
- The world
- The Kingdom

Having been a "follower" in both the nonprofit and for-profit sectors, I have compared the leadership of both and frankly found very little difference between the two. In all cases I performed at a much higher level, learned more and found much greater job satisfaction when following an *effective* leader.

In my comparison, the effectiveness of the leadership I was following always came back to the following leadership characteristics:

1. <u>The ability to identify and communicate reality</u>: They know precisely why the ministry exists, they communicate it and live it! They are always in pursuit of knowing the state of the health of the ministry. They are always asking: What works? What needs fixing? What should be abandoned? They allocate resources to accomplish what is required for success. They know the major donors who value and support the ministry at ministry-changing levels. They have a grasp of fundraising efforts at the big picture level and ensure their development team is highly effective.

2. <u>Decisive</u>: The problems and opportunities of the ministry are being grasped and acted upon in a timely manner. The CEO knows that s/he will NEVER have ALL the information necessary to make decisions, but s/he also knows when it's time to make the call.

3. <u>Can deal with conflict</u>: When conflicts arise (and they certainly will) both within and outside the ministry, they are acknowledged and resolved in a manner and timeframe that contributes to the health and vitality of the ministry in concert with the ministry's core values.

4. <u>The ability to convene</u>: A safe, orderly and productive environment is created for the respectful discussion of issues and ideas. S/he knows if this is not a personal strength. If it is not, someone else with this gifting is empowered to convene critical meetings.

5. <u>Seeks clarity</u>: All followers know what is expected of them. They know their responsibilities and are empowered with the authority to carry them out. Any requests for clarity are dealt within a reasonable amount of time.

6. <u>Maintains vigilance</u>: The overall health of the ministry is being cared for. Ministry relevance is cherished and nurtured. Problems and opportunities are identified and prepared for in time to allow for a proactive stance. Problems are proactively resolved to the benefit of the ministry.

7. <u>Highly curious</u>: Questions and active listening are greatly valued. Continual learning is practiced and encouraged. All new ideas will be heard and viable

ideas will be given serious consideration.

8. <u>High self-awareness</u>: The effective CEO is constantly monitoring his/her own strengths and weaknesses. S/he treasures and practices appropriate behavior while continually seeking to create an environment of trust, hope and inspiration.

9. <u>Exhibits excellent boundaries</u>: S/he has an innate sense of appropriate behavior both personally and corporately. Invasive or immature behaviors are immediately and appropriately challenged, knowing full well the impact they have on followers' ability to trust leadership.

10. <u>Continual pursuit of excellence</u>: Tradition and precedence are appropriately honored. S/he knows which traditions to keep and which to abandon. S/he knows the events of the past can be used as stepping-stones to the future on the path to corporate improvement.

11. <u>Ability to cast a vision for the ministry</u>: S/he understands the value of an achievable, articulated vision and knows that followers must have a clear understanding of where the organization is heading and why.

12. <u>Assures the existence of and adherence to the ministry's core values</u>: S/he knows what the ministry values in the way of appropriate behavior, culture and ultimate outcomes. The expressed core values are both modeled and administered with fairness and equity.

13. <u>Values competence and corporate health above personal loyalty</u>: S/he fully understands the toxic

nature of an "us and them" culture even to the point of choosing it over longstanding relationships. Is fully aware of the CEO's impact on followers and seeks to create an open and trusting community.

14. Understands the mission of the ministry includes ministry to the donors who fund it: Donors are seen and treated as key partners and recipients in ministry. Fundraising is embraced as a critical aspect of the ministry itself. S/he believes the ultimate blessing of giving belongs to the donor.

15. Serves through a "posture of indebtedness": Understands nothing is done or decided in a vacuum. The "lifting up" and empowering of others is the key to accomplishing the mission.

Able followership requires able leadership. Rule #59: *The effective CEO contributes to all that is good,* is more prevalent when board members are *actively committed* to the core values that lead to the health of the ministry's corporate culture. While, in my eyes, *policy* boards are more helpful to ministries than *administrative* boards, it is *always* appropriate for boards to monitor the overall health of the organizations they serve. **Only they can provide the corrective action needed at the highest levels to protect those who carry out the mission of the ministry.**

RULE #59
"An ineffective Chief Development Officer drains the life out of your ministry."

What I'm about to tell you REALLY happened. This tale is not *based* upon a true story; I'm sad to say it *is actually a VERY true story.*

One of my colleagues and I were spending the day with a ministry who had contracted with our firm to help them with their direct mail program. The meeting had been set for weeks, an agenda had been prepared in advance and had been agreed to by the ministry. As is our practice, we had arrived at their headquarters a few minutes early out of respect for the development team who was hosting us.

After a short wait in their reception area, we were ushered into their conference room and began to set up for the meeting. The president of the organization was the first to arrive. He stepped into the room and greeted us warmly, wished us well in our meeting with his team, and then he departed. A few minutes later, several members of his development staff began filing into the room with their agendas, coffee cups in hand and smiles on their faces. We shook hands, exchanged greetings, and everyone found a place to sit facing the screen where our PowerPoint presentation could be easily seen.

As meetings go, it was progressing fairly well. Ideas

were flowing, plans were being presented and discussed, modifications were being made, as needed, and decisions were being made.

We broke for lunch, which ran a little longer than expected, but hey, these things happen, so when we returned to the conference room we reviewed our progress against the agenda, deleted a couple of items that were of less importance and resumed our meeting.

Now this story begins to get a little weird. Around 2:30 in the afternoon one of the development staff stood up and left the room. This person didn't say anything like, "I'll be right back," or "I have an important phone call." The guy just left. I asked the Chief Development Officer (CDO) if we should wait for his colleague to return. "No, let's just continue," he said; so we did. In a few more minutes another member of the team departed in much the same manner. We just carried on. Soon someone else left, and by 3:00pm the CDO followed suit.

My colleague and I found ourselves sitting in the conference room with no one to talk to but each other. We exchanged glances and just sat there for about five minutes. Finally I whispered to my colleague, "Kind of quiet out there, isn't it?" He looked at the door leading to the hallway outside and said, "Yeah, kind of eerie, isn't it?" Another two minutes passed and I decided to go see what was going on...emerging from the conference room, I encountered an empty building! Absolutely no one was there!

I went back into the conference room and informed my colleague of the strangeness of our situation. "I guess the meeting's over. We might as well just pack up and leave too!"

As we left the building I could see the CDO climbing into his car way across the parking lot. He just waved! The only thing I could think to do, in the moment, was wave back! So we just drove to the airport and took a two-hour flight home...

While this is one of my strangest experiences as a fundraising consultant, I wish I could say this was a once-in-a-lifetime occurrence. This "disappearing act" occurred on several other occasions with this ministry.

During my tenure in the great halls of philanthropy, I've encountered many other situations that were quite disarming and disappointing. In each case, the Chief Development Officer stood at the center of the dysfunction.

I have also come to recognize that *most* Chief Development Officers are quite capable, and many are absolutely outstanding. But there are many, especially in smaller nonprofit organizations, who are ill-prepared for the responsibilities they carry. Unfortunately, in these cases the ministries suffer from serious lack of funding.

As you know, resources for the accomplishment of your mission are highly dependent upon this person. No resources; no impact. No impact; no ministry. Harsh words, to say the least. But true nonetheless. Here are just a few of the attributes of an *ineffective* CDO:

- *Interest,* but not *passion:* for your mission, ministry and donors
- Energy lags, except at 4:00pm, has a poor work ethic and does only the minimal requirements of the job
- People skills are wanting (can be reclusive, strident, insecure or insensitive)

- Has an acute lack of self-awareness
- Very limited communication skills
- A demonstrated ability to TALK about raising funds rather than actually DOING it
- A "personal theology or philosophy" that conflicts with Scripture and reality in general
- A high tendency to make assumptions rather than dig for the facts
- Is constantly in search of "the magic bullet" or idea that will turn everything around, e.g., spends much of their time on the things that produce the least results because they do not know the rules of fundraising
- Not a trusting delegator or, conversely, delegates everything
- Lacks the energy and curiosity to be constantly learning about the best practices of fundraising
- Takes credit for the effective work of others (runs to get ahead of the parade)

Very seldom have I seen a Chief Development Officer who exhibits ALL of these negative characteristics. They would most likely not be hired in the first place should this be the case. But if a CDO has several of these critically dysfunctional traits, s/he can cause great harm to a ministry. This is why Rule #59, *An ineffective Chief Development Officer drains the life out of your ministry,* is included here.

RULE #60
"An effective Chief Development Officer is a gift to the spirit!"

When I first met her, she was sitting in the office of the CEO. The ministry headquarters was housed in an old apartment building. Not much to look at, the apartments had been converted into offices (so just about everybody had their own bathroom)! This was a great benefit to the staff, but it was clearly not suitable for a ministry headquarters and a short-term solution at best for this critical ministry.

As I met with this Chief Development Officer (CDO) and the CEO for the very first time, I couldn't help but notice that buckets that were strategically placed all over the CEO's office. It had been raining for days, and the dripping of water from the ceiling was more than a little distracting as we began our discussions. The really telling thing about the state of this old structure was we were meeting in an office on the first floor of this two-story building! The rain had passed through the top floor and was leaking from the ceiling into the ground floor. I had a momentary concern about the ceiling caving in from the weight of the water but decided to push it out of my mind and continue our meeting.

There was a "chair rail" around the entire office with architectural drawings displaying a beautiful new headquarters as well as several other campuses intended to replace existing old structures currently in use by this historic ministry.

The CEO then motioned to all of the architectural drawings and said, "This is where we are going. What can you do to help us grow our number of donors so we can afford to operate in our new facilities once they are built?"

"How much more funding do you need?" I asked.

The CEO and CDO responded, in unison, "One million dollars net!"

"When will you need to achieve this increase in income?" I asked.

"Within the next five years," the CDO responded. "That's when we'll be fully operational."

I sat there and looked at the buckets, slowly filling with water. Then my gaze went back to the drawings. Once I refocused my eyes and fixed them upon these two people, I saw great faith and determination in their eyes.

"Would you like me to prepare a proposal for you?" I asked.

Then the CDO spoke. She said, "We aren't even sure that we can meet payroll this month, Doug. We're preparing a mailing, but I think we need help to do it right."

I looked at what they were preparing to mail and offered to help them, even as I worked on a proposal.

"We don't even know if we can afford you," said the CDO. I thought for a moment and said, "The money from this appeal will be generated before my invoice arrives."

"Really?" she said. "You think our little donor file of 3,000 people can generate enough money to pay you and have enough left to help with our payroll?"

I asked several more questions about the ministry, including what their current supporters liked to give to, and how the ministry was perceived by the community.

Their answers and determination gave me a sense of confidence that if we proceeded together, using the best practices of direct response fundraising (or the rules of fundraising, if you will), we would be successful in helping to grow this vital ministry.

My proposal, when presented, had been modest but also laid out a plan for significant growth through acquiring new donors while cultivating their existing supporters. The CEO had also asked for a five-year-plan to generate the additional $1 million in net for ministry. In faith, they accepted my proposal, and the work began in earnest.

My initial mailing had indeed produced the expected income and then some. Their little group of donors were proving to be quite generous and committed when asked in an appropriate way.

Over the next several weeks, months and years I met with the CDO as often as the situation required. She was always prepared with many questions, which I appreciated, since many CDOs approach fundraising with their assumptions as opposed to questions. But she also brought many other desirable traits to our partnership. Here are just a few of the attributes of an effective CDO:

- Passion: for your mission, ministry, donors and life in general
- Knows, understands and embraces the financial goals of the ministry

- Has great energy, enough to fill a stadium
- Has a very high degree of self-awareness
- People skills that are wonderfully infectious to all around them
- A spirit of curiosity about what motivates donors to give
- A commitment to life-long learning about fundraising
- Is constantly aware of the ministry's financial needs, goals and progress toward achieving them from all sources
- Fully understands that income and expense are inextricably linked (see *The Rules of Fundraising,* Rule #16)
- A demonstrated ability to raise funds (usually through major donors)
- Exhibits clear and established boundaries with donors
- Has sound judgment in deciding what opportunities to pursue or decline
- A clearly intelligent person who leads the development team
- A collaborator with their peers, who doesn't have to know all the answers
- Has trusting relationships with the leadership team, CEO and board
- Believes in trusted partnerships with consultants (rather than seeing them as vendors)
- A trusting delegator
- Embraces the media as a friend to the ministry and cultivates them accordingly
- Gives credit where credit is due

To sum up the characteristics of a highly effective Chief Development Officer, it can be said of them that s/he is a master craftsman of the great profession of philanthropic encouragement to all they encounter.

The CDO of the ministry I described at the beginning of this rule had most of the attributes listed immediately above. She had many of them when I met her. Over time, I saw her acquire many more of these traits as the ministry grew.

Little did I realize, that first day, in the leaky office, that I would participate in and witness all that this ministry would become. Today it is one of the largest, most highly effective and respected ministries in one of the largest cities in the United States!

The CDO, who is now retired, was the very epitome of Rule #60, *An effective Chief Development Officer is a gift to the spirit!* I'm certain she will hear, "Well done, good and faithful servant."

NOTES:

RULE #61

"CFOs rule the world (or at least the country you live in)."

Early in my days as a CEO of my own company, the first thing my CFO said to me was, "My first responsibility is to keep you out of jail!" I assure you, he received my complete attention!

As we progressed in our relationship, I came to realize my CFO was NOT implying that he was an attorney. He was helping me to better realize that, like it or not, I had a business partner, Uncle Sam and his colleagues, the Internal Revenue Service (IRS).

Now, I hadn't asked for this partnership, and, if given an option, I wouldn't seek to go into business with the state and federal governments. But let's face it, whoever said, "The only thing that's certain is death and taxes," wasn't kidding! We are all mortal, and if we want to continue a life of freedom, we are all taxpayers. And just to add insult to injury, the government gets paid first!

In good years, after taxes, my company is a for-profit entity. But this book is largely written for those working in the not-for-profit sector, and according to the laws of our land, your ministry or organization is likely tax-exempt. It has been determined that if your organization meets the requirements of the government, the institution you work for is not required to pay taxes. And it gets even better! Those who decide to support your organization are able to deduct the amount of their gifts to the full extent of the law! It is very encouraging to know, at the time of writing, we live in a land that reinforces giving to charitable causes. I am grateful for this and do not take it for granted.

According to the Internal Revenue Service, here in the U.S.:

"The most common type of tax-exempt nonprofit organization falls under category 501(c)(3), whereby a nonprofit organization is exempt from federal income tax if its activities have the following purposes: charitable, religious, educational, scientific, literary, testing for public safety, fostering amateur sports competition, or preventing cruelty to children or animals."

In Canada, according to Corporationcentre.ca:

"A non-profit corporation is a legal entity separate from its members and directors formed for purposes other than generating a profit to be distributed to its members, directors or officers as dividends. While a non-profit corporation can earn a profit, the profit must be used to further the goals of the corporation rather than to pay dividends to its membership. Non-profit corporations are formed pursuant to federal or provincial law. A non-profit corporation can be a church or church association, school, charity, activity clubs, volunteer services organization, professional association, research institute, museum, or in some cases, a sports association. Non-profit corporations must apply for charitable status to benefit from tax-exempt status and be able to issue tax deductible receipts to donors."

So, if your organization is granted tax-exempt status from the federal, state and provincial government, why do CFOs rule the world in a not-for-profit environment?

The short answer is, because the government looks to your corporate financial statements to provide compliance with the laws...not reports compiled by the development department.

As a fundraiser, all of your critically necessary reports and analyses are tools you need to use to be the most effective craftsman you can be. Personally and professionally I stand with you on this. But alas, ours is a world of communications and philanthropy...not accounting. So, it's totally conceivable if a certain amount of tension or, taken to the extreme, even resentment can build between the accounting department and those responsible for development.

This tension usually becomes exaggerated when income to your ministry falls short of expectations. I can assure you, I've been in the meetings when the income is below projections. It usually goes something like this:

The leadership team is meeting and the various officers are going around the conference table reporting on their areas of responsibility. You are seated somewhere near the folks who are delivering services (for some reason they appear to have a higher level of compassion). The order of presentation is predetermined by the CEO, and it's been printed on the agenda. As so often occurs, your report is slated immediately following the finance report. When the development department income is at or ahead of projections, this is generally a non-event. When the income is *below* projections, it really becomes a matter of *how far below?*

If you're like me, when I was the Vice President of Development in a nonprofit, you feel personally responsible for achieving or exceeding your department's income goals. When the numbers are significantly below projections, you feel as though you've let the ministry down. Flushed faces, sweaty palms, and feelings of inadequacy often become the norm for development officers at a time like this. Again, if you're like me, it may even be hard for you to make eye contact with the other members of the Leadership Team.

What I'm about to say now are the *critical keys* to being able to look your colleagues directly in the eye:

1. Intimate knowledge of your annual plan and budget
2. Highly developed relationships with your CFO and CEO
3. Constant communication with your CFO and CEO
4. Expert preparation for your leadership team meeting
5. Bringing *full disclosure* AND *solutions*

If you have indeed done the above, the outcome of your report to the team could be as straightforward as:

1. A major gift of, let's say, $500,000 was expected this month, but the donor called and explained it took them

longer than expected to receive the proceeds of the sale of their business, so the gift will be delayed by a month.

2. The recent natural disaster on the Gulf Coast has received significant media attention, and all income areas are down. Your development team has prepared an emergency strategy to offset the shortfall, and you expect income to be brought within 90% of projections within the next 60 days (be prepared to discuss your strategies in detail, complete with handouts or visuals showing all assumptions).

A highly skilled development officer is going to understand and value the role of a CFO in her organization. Seldom have I ever encountered a CFO who didn't want the very same things I wanted as a development officer, i.e., for the ministry to prosper financially. For this reason, I recommend that you include your CFO in the budgeting and planning process of your department. Yes, this helps the CFO to be able to feel invested in your department's plans. It also does something of perhaps greater importance. It gives you the benefit of their institutional knowledge. It also provides a financially experienced second set of eyes to review and the opportunity for them to ask questions during the planning process rather than at the leadership team meeting. An involved CFO is a happy CFO. And what's not to like about that? After all, as this rule states, *CFOs rule the world!*

NOTES:

RULE #62
"Opportunities can be very expensive."

It was a black tie evening. Everyone was glittering and coifed as they mingled with what author Tom Wolfe would have described as, "The Masters of the Universe." A small orchestra played classic big-band tunes as people circulated and eventually made their way to their assigned tables. The centerpieces and place settings were beautiful and would have made Martha Stewart proud.

Out in the adjacent hallway a silent auction was equally well presented with amazing gifts and weekend getaway opportunities. Being a fundraising consultant, and an invited guest, I started the bidding on several of these tantalizing trophies, all the while hoping someone would outbid me so I wouldn't have to come up with the cash. My more altruistic motive was to see this well-known organization generate significant funding for their great work for children in need.

As I found my own seat at the table, I found myself wondering just how much this evening of grandeur was going to cost this worthwhile charity.

Sometime during dinner, a woman in a black sequined dress approached the microphone. The band played to a slow stop, and the woman began addressing the guests gathered around the 100 tables in the banquet hall. It was all so very grand and lovely! But there was something wrong. I couldn't hear what our hostess was saying! I could tell she was thanking everyone for coming, and she stepped aside for what I assumed was a representative of the charity. But I couldn't hear her either. She spoke for less than three minutes. She didn't even show a short video. Everyone applauded and then went back to the prime rib, chicken cordon bleu or the fish that they had chosen from their invitations.

From time to time people would excuse themselves and go out into the hallway to see how they were faring on their bids for signed baseballs, autographed guitars and bed-and-breakfast packages.

Conversations continued around the tables during dessert until the hostess reappeared at the microphone and had the band play a "call to order." She again expressed her appreciation for all those who were taking time out of their busy schedules to attend the evening's festivities. Straining to hear, I guessed she must have announced that the bidding would close soon, because several people made hurried visits to the silent auction and returned to their tables, whispering something into the ear of their spouses or dates.

The remainder of the evening included more music and dancing, and then, long after I was ready to make my escape (tuxedos and I don't do well together), the winners of the silent auction were announced. It was a very long list of items, so this took close to an hour. Again, the sound system prevented me from hearing much of what was said. I know somebody must have been able to hear, because with each announcement a table would erupt as the happy winner beamed and was patted on the back in congratulations.

I tell this tale to illustrate Rule #62: *Opportunities can be very expensive.* In this case the financial cost was likely significant. I don't know the net income generated from this annual gala, because I was in attendance as a guest rather than my usual role as consultant. But what I DO know is the enormous amount of work that goes into something like this.

Even if volunteers perform much of the work, there is still an inordinate amount of time required by the staff of any charity that attempts to fund their event solely by a silent auction. Now, as I mentioned, the items auctioned were quite expensive. But so was the opulence of the evening. I came away thinking that this annual event was primarily an opportunity for couples to have a night of dining and dancing for what they perceived was a good cause.

I'm aware that I run the risk of sounding like a curmudgeon, but, to this fundraiser, it felt like the expense of the evening could have been used in far more profitable ways. In addition to what appeared to be a relatively low return on investment, I was saddened that I attended this event and came away without hearing what the mission of the organization was and how they were making a difference in the lives of children in need.

The Chronicle of Philanthropy, a high quality trade journal for the fundraising community, published an issue in March of 2016 entitled: "Killing Sacred Cows." It featured three case studies of nonprofits that had improved their bottom line income by moving away from historic forms of fundraising.

It not only caught my eye, but it reminded me of my own attendance at this charity gala. If your organization is currently engaged in fundraising activities that eat your time and deliver low returns, you may want to visit *Philanthropy.com* and see how several discerning nonprofits learned to turn away from opportunities that were not delivering at the highest possible levels.

Every opportunity to raise funds comes with a price tag in both dollars and time. Learning what to embrace and what to refuse requires wisdom and experience. It's my hope that you will find highly profitable strategies to further your own mission!

RULE #63
"True innovation is very hard to find."

There's an old joke that never seems to lose its savor: "What's the best way to outrun a bear? Go hiking in the woods with a slow friend." Not a bad joke, especially when you realize that the fastest bear is a black bear, which can run up to 60 kilometers per hour, which, according to Reference.com, is approximately 37 miles per hour. The fastest recorded human running speed, as of 2014, was the great Jamaican Olympian Usain Bolt, who achieved 27.44 miles per hour. To my way of thinking, this means I should never hit the trail with Usain, or most other people for that matter. Do I need to say I'm NOT a runner? In fact, there are a lot of things I'm not. But I don't spend much time thinking about those things. We fundraisers, who are neurotics, have other important things to worry about, like how to come up with new ideas for raising money.

I suppose, if I were to apply the logic of the bear joke, I could believe that I don't need new ideas, I just need to have more ideas than those who hire me as their fundraising consultant. But that's not the way I'm wired. The way I figure it, God created me to do what I love. I am truly blessed to know what I have a passion for and what I have the talent to accomplish. He fashioned me into a fundraiser, to be part of what is *right* with the world. Since you're reading this, I sense we are kindred spirits in the art and craft of helping people to give in order to save and change lives.

If we're going to outrun the bear without sacrificing our friends, we're going to need new ways of thinking, a spirit of innovation, if you will. But as this rule states, "True innovation is very hard to find." At face value I find this rule quite intimidating. I find myself asking, "What does it take to truly innovate?" "Why is innovation so difficult?" "Am I even capable of innovation?"

Thankfully I stumbled across a great book, *Innovate Like Edison: The Success System of America's Greatest Inventor*, written by Michael J. Gelb and Sarah Miller Caldicott, who is a great grandniece of Thomas Edison. So this book is about Thomas Edison, the light bulb guy, the phonograph guy, the moving pictures guy and the guy who invented so many other incredible and complex innovations that impact us all today.

The authors have done us all a favor by helping us better understand Edison as a person as well as America's greatest inventor and innovator. Their intent, as I understand it, is to teach a system of thought and action. But, being somewhat of a CliffsNotes guy, I found myself attracted to and comforted by many of the inspiring pullout quotes from Edison and many other amazingly talented leaders in their fields, such as:

"Every organization—not just business—needs one core competence: innovation."

Peter Drucker

"I start where the last man left off."
Thomas Edison

"I see what has been accomplished at great labor and expense in the past. I gather the data of many thousands of experts as a starting point and then I make thousands more."
Thomas Edison

"Every adversity, every failure, every heartache carries with it the seed of an equal or greater benefit."
Napoleon Hill

"Cherish your visions and your dreams, as they are the children of your soul, the blueprints of your ultimate achievements."
Napoleon Hill

"Patience, persistence and perspiration make an unbeatable combination for success."
Napoleon Hill

Gelb and Caldicott provide us with a critical insight that is often overlooked in testing or experimenting while innovating in fundraising:

"At an early age, Edison trained himself to view the outcomes of his experiments as "neutral" rather than negative or positive. He recognized that each experiment brought him one step closer to the answers he sought. By maintaining an objective viewpoint, Edison analyzed his findings without an agenda, applying the broadest possible applications of his results, thus yielding insights that would otherwise have been unavailable to him. The ability to look at one's self and one's circumstances objectively is a profoundly valuable tool for personal fulfillment and success. And, the ability to be a rigorously objective observer of your data is absolutely essential to the innovator." (Page 76)

A final word from Edison before we move on:

"My philosophy of life is work—bringing out the secrets of nature and applying them for the happiness of man. I know of no better service to render during the short time we are in this world."

Thomas Alva Edison

As people of faith who labor in the fields of philanthropy, there is still so much to learn about our craft and better still to contribute to the body of knowledge that moves us all forward in our endeavors as we seek to save and change the lives of people created in the image of God.

Innovation in fundraising requires the same attributes Edison employed, researching all that has gone before, experimenting relentlessly, being totally convinced that failure is one more step toward success, which is entirely attainable.

If you're in any way like me, and find the word "innovation" a bit intimidating, it might be a comfort to realize what innovation ISN'T. Innovation is NOT creating something "ex nihilo," which is Latin for "out of nothing." The only person I have ever encountered, in my life, who could do this is the Creator. He created our entire universe by just speaking it into existence (see Genesis 1). Thankfully we are not being tasked, as innovators, to be the Creator. What we ARE being tasked with is to:

1. Research *everything* we can get our hands on that relates to the kind of fundraising we want to accomplish. While this isn't easy, it is a magnificent starting point that anyone can do!

2. Use all of the research you've compiled to begin asking questions. Following Edison's example, prohibit yourself and your colleagues from making assumptions. Assumptions are antithetical to true innovation. They will cause you to skip over critical information or data that may well lead you into the frustration of heading down the wrong path ending in an unfruitful journey.

3. Use your questions to begin developing a platform of "testing theories." Even these theories should be postulated in the form of questions, e.g., "I wonder what would happen if I printed out the gift histories of my top 50 donors?"

4. Looking at these giving histories, what do I see?

This might be a good time to share a story I first heard while attending my science class in college. I was terrified of science. Just the mere mention of chemistry gave me hives. So I looked through the selection of science classes available that looked the least threatening. I settled on earth science taught by Dr. Solomon Raju.

He was a wonderfully warm man, standing no more than 5'6", wearing a white lab coat. He spoke in such soft and soothing tones that my hives began to dissipate a little. He began our first class with a precious gift. It was a story paraphrased from Samuel H. Scudder's *Look at Your Fish*. You can find this story in its complete written form by simply typing "Look at Your Fish" into Google.

Dr. Raju told his version of the story this way:

"A science student sat down at a table in the laboratory and waited for the famous professor Agassiz to begin his class. He didn't begin with any great and memorable lecture. But what he did do surprised the student. He was instructed to open a jar, containing a specimen of a fish. The student was to lay it on a tray in front of him and look at it. Doing as instructed the student sat on the stool, the fish before him, and looked down at the fish. Once he had done this he looked up at Professor Agassiz awaiting his next instruction. The professor motioned with his hand and simply repeated his original instruction, "Look at the fish." So the obedient student looked down at the fish." Every time he looked up, the professor would motion again and repeat the words, "Look at the fish." Then the professor left the room. The student looked around briefly and then bent his head down to further examine the fish. He began to see things he had not seen at first glance, like the shape of the scales, the number of fins, the sharpness of the teeth, the color of the specimen. The longer he looked the more he began to see."

Then my earth science professor, Dr. Raju, opened his arms widely and then said, "This is science, looking at the fish to really see what is there. That's what we'll be doing in this class!"

This simple story, or parable, if you will, can guide you as you begin examining the gift histories of your top 50 donors. When I took this approach, here are a few of the things that I began to see:

1.   The donors' names
2.   The dates on which they gave their gifts
3.   The amounts they gave each time
4.   What they gave to
5.   What mechanism or channel they used to give

To my delight I began to see patterns:

1.   The gender of the donor(s)
2.   Many of the donors gave quarterly.
3.   Some of the donors gave annually.
4.   Several of the donors gave monthly.
5.   Gift sizes varied greatly, except the monthly donors who were very consistent in their gift amounts.
6.   Several of the largest givers often skipped a year between gifts or at the very least were inconsistent in their frequency of giving.
7.   The vast majority of the non-monthly donors gave only in the 4th quarter of the year.

8. A few donors had given $10,000 a year but then broke pattern and gave $50,000 or some other large gift, but did so one time only.

By looking closely I began to realize that I needed to let the donor's giving history inform my strategies for asking for gifts. Why would I ask a donor, whose pattern indicated she was clearly a 4th quarter giver, for an Easter gift?

Soon I began applying this same kind of examination to the rest of the donors on the donor list. It helped me to determine when to present the right offers, to the right donors, at the right times, using the right channels! How exciting! The mysteries of innovation were beginning to make themselves more visible to me.

As this rule states, *"True innovation is very hard to find."* The common threads found amongst the innovators I've known or studied include some traits worth restating:

1. Be willing to do work others will not.
2. Never give up.
3. Ask questions rather than making assumptions.
4. Learn what others have done and build upon it.
5. Look at the fish.

Happy fishing!

RULE #64
"Strategy drives EVERYTHING!"

Dictionary.com gives several definitions for the word strategy. I like the fourth definition the best, especially in the context of fundraising:

"A plan, method or series of maneuvers or stratagems for obtaining a specific goal or result: a strategy for getting ahead in the world."

Sounds straightforward enough, if we'd just do it. But many of us give in to the temptation to forget about the "goal" part of strategic thinking and leap right into tactics. Which is defined a little differently (again I prefer the fourth definition): "of or pertaining to arrangement or order; tactical."

The journeymen fundraisers I've known throughout my career all knew the difference between "strategy" and "tactics." It's part of what made them so great in the workshop of philanthropy.

Knowing this key difference isn't limited to fundraising by any means. It might better illustrate this rule by looking at another field of expertise...

Recently I bought a home, here where I live, in the Midwest. It is a 1955 ranch-style house with a full basement. It is a very well-maintained place, had recently been updated, and didn't have ANY evidence of a leaky basement...until the heavy summer rains began. During a booming Saturday thunderstorm, about six inches of rain fell. I went down to the basement to check on some laundry and, much to my chagrin, I noticed water pooling out from under my storage room door. Of course my storage room was filled with cardboard boxes.

Mayhem ensued as I moved dripping boxes, old furniture and everything else that was sitting on the floor out into the dry part of my basement. I ran next door, borrowed my neighbor's Wet-Vac, and began sucking up about 75 gallons of water. Way back in a hard-to-get-to corner, I noticed water coming into the basement. I made a hurried call to a well-known basement sealing company who informed me it was going to be two days before anyone could even look at it.

On the day John, the basement guy, arrived, he politely introduced himself, asked if he could come in, and then placed those funny-looking blue booties over his shoes before entering.

Down in the basement he turned on his flashlight, carefully examining the suspected source of water. Then he did something STRATEGIC! He said, "Well...it's dry now, so I guess we have to make it leak!" I was greatly impressed. He didn't just take my word for where I had seen water bubbling in; he went outside, took my garden hose and placed it right up against the foundation, and let it run.

In about five minutes the white paint in the corner began turning dark as the water worked its way underneath the paint about a foot above where I had seen the bubbling. John used a scraper to expose an amateur patch job under the paint. A few days later the crack was properly sealed.

About six months later, another storm and more water appeared. Scrambling ensued, boxes were moved, another call was made. This time it wasn't John who came. The man diagnosed the problem by identifying a large crack that COULD be the source, and recommended several expensive repairs, including replacing my entire basement floor! The repairman just assumed the large crack was the problem. After the man left I immediately called John's cell phone directly. He came over very quickly and carefully examined the grade of my yard and made sensible recommendations. I had the repairs made and have had no other issues.

John didn't guess. He made no assumptions. He was thorough in his examination and realized the continuing problem wasn't the large crack *inside* my basement but rather groundwater management *outside* the house!

John knew the goal was to keep water out of my basement. His colleague assumed that if we did several rather expensive things, it would seal the basement. The reality is, if I had done those things, the water problem would have continued. He was looking at the wrong things because he had not done the work to determine *why* the water was coming into the basement. He just wanted to fill cracks! He was guessing in his diagnosis. He was just interested *how* to plug the inside of the house.

As fundraisers, we can't afford to guess either. We owe it to ourselves and the ministries we represent to do our work based upon proven principles or rules. Like John, we need to think *strategically* rather than *tactically*. Strategy requires that we know *what* we're trying to accomplish (raise more net dollars for ministry). Tactics are the actions or *how* we'll carry out our strategy (like which fundraising channels to use).

Less experienced fundraisers tend to start their efforts by identifying a channel or tactic, e.g., "let's do an email to our donors asking for $200,000 for our general fund." A more experienced fundraiser will ask, "What is the likelihood that our donors will give to this kind of project?" These are VERY different questions, which will yield VERY different results.

To put an even finer point on it, a strategic approach to the need for $200,000 in general operating funds should lead to several questions (rather than assumptions):

1. Have we ever approached our donors for general fund money before? If so, what were the results? Were they acceptable?

2. How have we successfully raised general fund monies in the past?

3. Are there "more donor attractive" projects being paid for by our general fund?

4. Do we need $200,000 for those more donor attractive projects? If not, how much DO we need?

5. If we don't have $200,000 in more donor attractive projects, do we have enough need to justify an appeal?

6. Do we have *successful* tactics we have employed in raising general funds? If so, what are the numbers?

7. What was the "offer" we used when we last raised money for our general fund?

8. Have we ever tested annual fund offers for general fund money? Results?

9. What channels would be most effective in raising money for our general fund?

Developing solid strategies beats out "channel-guessing" every time. That's why Rule #64, *Strategy drives EVERYTHING,* is so critical to the success of your development program.

NOTES:

RULE #65
"Fundraising is relational science"

When I began my journey into fundraising in 1980, I remember how surprised I was at all of the numbers involved. It sounds pretty naïve and a bit silly today just writing this. But if you had walked in my shoes up to this point, it may make more sense to you:

I was sitting in my 8th grade Algebra II class at Morgan Junior High in Ellensburg, Washington. My teacher was up at the chalkboard writing out yet another formula. My head began to throb, and a great knot began forming in my stomach. I was beginning to feel the deep depression that washed over me whenever he did this.

I felt like I was a complete and utter failure.

Looking around the classroom, I noticed most of my fellow students were watching carefully as the instructor continued to write a series of marks that involved punctuation, letters and numbers. Most of them seemed to be tracking with him. But I certainly wasn't! I found my mind wandering...

I saw young Abraham Lincoln lying by the fireplace in his log cabin; he was writing words on the back of the wooden shovel that was used to remove ashes from the firebox. He was too poor to buy any paper, so he scratched his letters into the soot-covered shovel. The flames of the fire provided enough light for him to see...

"Mr. Shaw!"

My head jerked up at the commanding voice of my teacher!

"Yes...?" was all I could whisper, knowing I had once again been caught not paying attention.

"Come up here right now!" he commanded, motioning to his desk.

I was kind of dizzy as I stood up. My cheeks were burning with embarrassment as I steadied myself with one hand on my desk. Then I began the "walk of shame" up to face the teacher's waiting glare.

"Mr. Shaw, do you want to be in this class?" he barked.

"No...no, I do not," I squeaked out, much to my own surprise.

"Well, Mr. Shaw, you had better get your head in the game!" he commanded.

"I...I don't want to take algebra. I just don't get it," I stammered, hoping my pants were still dry.

"Well, if you don't take algebra, you will be slamming the door of life in your face!" he yelled as he stood up from his desk.

I didn't know how to respond. So I didn't. I just stood there shaking.

"Go to the office!" he said, while quickly filling out a hall pass

He thrust it toward me, and I grabbed it like a condemned man. Spinning on my heels, I made for the door. I couldn't get out of there fast enough! If I slammed the door behind me it wasn't intentional. I just wanted to get away from this frightening man with his contemptuous glare. I knew I could never face him or my classmates again.

Now, my final experience with math, during my formal education, came on a winter's day while I was in my in junior year attending Oroville High School, way up in the Okanagan Valley of Washington State. It was a tiny mountain town on the Canadian border. The snows always came early there.

The flakes of the first snow of the year had just begun falling as I gazed out the window of my Geometry II class. My teacher was at the chalkboard drawing trapezoids or something. When I turned my head back to the front of the class I could tell he was watching me.

He was a quiet little man, who wore a bowtie and looked very much like what a math teacher should look like to me. This time, there was no public humiliation involved. He simply waited for the bell to ring and then walked up to my desk.

"Doug," he said quietly, "What would you say if I offered you a D- for the class and you take another course that you find more interesting?"

I perked up immediately, "Really?" I responded hopefully. "You'd do that?"

"Yes," he said. "This clearly isn't for you."

"Do you want me to continue attending class until the end of the quarter?" I inquired.

"There's no need," he said compassionately. "You can take study hall. I'll still give you a passing grade."

"Fantastic!" I replied enthusiastically. My heart soared as I left the classroom. I felt like a hangman's noose had just been lifted from my 17-year-old neck!

The year was 1969, and back then, a D- was still considered

a passing grade.

It's now October 24, 2016, as I write this. It's the 22nd anniversary of my company, Douglas Shaw & Associates. And I find it quite amazing that I have spent my entire adult career totally and joyfully engaged in an industry that measures EVERYTHING...in numbers!

In fundraising we measure things like:

- Response rates
- Average gift size
- Retention rates
- Test results
- Donor trending
- Income forecasting
- Lifetime value of donors (five-year net value)
- Net yield per thousand (net dollars per one thousand donors)

In fact, I'm fond of saying in fundraising we measure "everything that wiggles."

How could a guy who quit Algebra II and narrowly escaped Geometry II with a D- have a successful career in fundraising? Sometimes I wonder at this myself.

Here's what I've decided:

Math for math's sake doesn't hold my interest. But numbers that have tangible relevance absolutely intrigue me! I LOVE knowing the exact gift amounts of a highly effective appeal that will save lives and change the lives of women, men and children. For this fundraiser, this is what matters most.

Because of Rule #65: *Fundraising is Relational Science,* it's prudent that I also speak to the *relational* aspects of this marriage of these two critical disciplines.

As veteran fundraisers know, donors are not moved to give when they simply read or hear statistics. Donors need a *context* for their giving. Just as I have shared some of my own story with you, donors need to know the stories of how their giving is accomplishing lasting and eternal change in the lives of people in need.

The ancient art of storytelling is something we all still love and need. A good story holds us captive; it makes us feel, think, cheer and sometimes mourn. We are indeed fortunate in that we live in an age when we can choose how we will hear or watch great storytelling through our Kindles, smartphones, iPads, computers, and good old standbys like theatre, cinema, books, radio and television. In fundraising we use direct mail, newsletters, online, video and special events, plus many other emerging forms of communication. But in all of these delivery systems, it's still the quality of the stories that captivates imaginations.

We all know fundraising is measured in numbers, but it is numbers generated by our abilities to motivate caring people to action through the tangible proof of true stories. Just as a good storyteller has to know his audience and tell his story in a manner that will be best received by his listeners, fundraisers must know their audiences too, delivering carefully crafted true stories to the right donor, asking for an appropriate gift using motivational language construction, i.e., a proven fundraising offer that inspires giving.

It is this ability to marry a good *relational* story, one that elicits emotion, to all of the knowledge of proven or *scientific* methods of fundraising, i.e., proven "offer construction" and database selections that will yield the results we're seeking. The challenge we all face is to do this without leaving the donor feeling guilty or manipulated, but inspired and exultant for doing what is good and what is in keeping with their values. You'll find all of this effort is worth your while when you experience the deepening relationships with your donors that come from employing this Rule #65: *Fundraising is Relational Science.*

RULE #66

"First do no harm (making changes to your development program)."

You don't have to be around the halls of philanthropy very long to see what happens when there's a significant leadership change in a ministry. I usually see the phenomena I'm about to describe when a new CEO is named or there is a change in Chief Development Officer (CDO).

To put it simply, the reason for the change in CEO is that somebody left. The specific circumstances vary, but there's a vacancy and it must be filled. The CDO position maybe also be the result of a departure or a newly formed position. When positions are filled, from within or outside the organization, changes occur.

Many years ago I was working for a medium-sized rescue mission on the west coast. The current CEO had been called back in from retirement in order to buy the board more time to recruit a new CEO. He also had several health issues and wanted to relinquish his position as soon as possible.

The board conducted a national search and settled on a much younger leader, Joe, who showed much promise and drive. He was referred by a trusted association leader but was not well-known locally.

My firm was providing the mission with fundraising

consulting services at the time, and we were now facing a transition of leadership. During my first meeting with Joe, he informed me that it was his intent to NOT make ANY changes for his first six months. He wanted to see how the ministry was doing, make his own evaluation, and then consider any changes that might need to occur.

I remember leaving Joe's office thinking, "This guy is DYING to change as much as he can as fast as he can." He had to stifle himself several times during our meeting, because he kept identifying problems everywhere he looked. Even his body language indicated he was fighting to control himself. He reminded me of a racehorse quivering in his gate just before the start of a race.

What alarmed me the most during my first meeting with Joe was his demand that my firm not serve any other not-for-profit in his city. He, for his part, committed to informing me months in advance should he consider changing fundraising agencies.

Within 30 days of Joe's arrival, I received a FedEx envelope containing a contract termination letter. I was absolutely stunned! I felt hurt, betrayed and angry at Joe's decision. He did not even have the courtesy to have a cover letter explaining his action. I immediately picked up the phone and called Joe. He answered, and all he could say to my reminder of his verbal demands during our initial meeting was, "I know." Then he hung up.

After a few hours of reflection, consternation and fulmination, I decided to do something I have never done before or since. I made another phone call, this time to his board chair. He was stunned too! He had not been consulted or informed of the decision. He promised to investigate and call me back.

When the board chair and I spoke again the next day, he was very apologetic, saying, "I'm sorry to have to tell you that Joe has already signed a contract with another agency."

I wish I could tell you that this story ended well.

I wasn't to learn the extent of what had occurred until about three years later, when the new CEO of this same rescue mission contacted me. He was inquiring about my interest in coming to talk with him about signing a contract with him.

Joe, as it turned out, had stood the entire mission on its head, firing most of the senior staff, alienating many of the ministry's major donors and most of the community leaders in his town as well. The new CEO had been recruited from within the community and was well-known as a highly competent, visionary leader.

The development department had been driven out by Joe's erratic behavior. Most of the senior people had resigned, leaving only a faithful skeleton crew to attempt to hold things together. The ministry was suffering great losses in income and needed assistance right away to turn things around.

Granted, this is a VERY extreme case, thankfully one I have never seen repeated in its far-reaching effects. Trust had been broken at so many different levels; lives had been disrupted and many careers were damaged.

What I HAVE seen repeated, all too often, are indiscriminate and uninformed changes to development programs by new leaders who want to make their mark, have jumped to conclusions, or perhaps just didn't know any better.

It's a good lesson for us all to remember Rule #66: *First do no harm (making changes to your development program)*.

Most of us generally think of this well-used phrase in the context of medicine. The Latin phrase, *Primum non nocere,* was first thought to be part of The Hippocratic Oath. The medical community has come to see that the origin of this profound statement is uncertain, but the point is not lost.

For our purposes, perhaps we should think of it as "use prudence" in making changes to your current development program.

To the overly cautious, it may also be misinterpreted as "leave everything alone; we might make a mistake." To the experienced fundraiser, it carries a different connotation.

Fundraising craftsmen have come to realize that to do nothing will accomplish just that, "nothing." To advance your mission, you will need to make some *strategic* changes in your approach to your donors. This is where it helps to know where others have trod the path before you.

I encourage leaders, upon entering a new assignment, to engage in discovery. *Discovery* is, after all, a great word. Here I like the dictionary's third definition:

"Law. Compulsory disclosure, as of facts or documents."

When attorneys take on a new case, they engage in discovery to determine the *facts* of a case. As fundraisers, we're doing the same thing. We're looking for:

1. What are our goals?
2. How is our ministry performing against these goals?
3. What's working and why?

4. What's not working and why?
5. What should be left alone and why?
6. What should be changed and why?
7. What changes should be made? How do we know?

This is where knowing the rules of fundraising is essential. This is why they've been compiled for your use. If you know something needs to be changed but are uncertain of what to do, you'll need to ask for help from a trusted source. There is no shame in asking for input or help. We all need it. None of us knows all of the rules, but there are colleagues in our industry who have great experience. One of the attributes I applaud in our philanthropic community is the spirit of generosity amongst development officers. The very nature of our work attracts people with generous spirits. And you can be a generous spirit to others who need help from you. But... *"first do no harm!"*

NOTES:

RULE #67
"Spend as much as you need to raise money."

Is this rule not heresy? Should we not be about the task of spending the *least* amount of money possible? After all, we need to be good stewards of the resources entrusted to us by our donors as they are prompted to give by our Creator.

This is all good thinking, but to my way of thinking, it is also incomplete. Seasoned fundraisers know that we need to spend the least amount of money possible *to accomplish our mission*. After all, mission is everything. But those who have been around the barn a few times also know that since accomplishing our mission is paramount, we should expend every effort and dollar on efforts that *we know* will propel our mission forward.

Now, I'm not living in some alternate reality here. I've lived and worked in the nonprofit community for most of my life. I'm fully aware that we all have financial constraints that must be recognized.

What this rule is saying is, *"Focus your attention on accomplishing your mission rather than on how to spend less money."* Let me give you an example:

One evening I was having dinner with the CEO of a longtime "ministry partner" (I prefer this language to calling those we serve "clients." It's more in keeping with my theology that whether we are working in a not-for-profit or a for-profit organization, we're advancing the kingdom, and we are all in ministry).

Our waiter had just served our entrees when the CEO looked me in the eyes and said, "We've just received $10 million dollars, and I want to spend it with you, if you can convince me it will help us in accomplishing our mission."

When was the last time you heard a CEO say these words? I never have! Not in ALL my years as a professional fundraiser. I blinked, swallowed, and then said, "Congratulations on receiving the $10 million! I think we can do something with that!" Now, this CEO is a true visionary, but he is so much more. He is ABSOLUTELY PASSIONATE about accomplishing what the Lord has called him to do.

So, what's happened since that eventful dinner?

This CEO has been a very active participant in what God is doing to totally revolutionize the translation of His Word into the languages of those who have never had the Scriptures in their own language.

Did this leader send me a check for $10 million dollars? No. He would never do that. But he did something just as bold. He has led the ministry by standing convention on its head. How did he do this?

Every waking moment has been spent finding new ways to accomplish the mission of this dynamic ministry. The entire organization is transfixed on accomplishing what God has called them to do. They are ALWAYS in search of new and better ways to not only accomplish their goals but to EXCEED them!

This commitment includes the development department. Together, we are continually testing new approaches to dramatically increase the ministry's donor file. When something works, they authorize significant resources in order to conduct even larger tests (to ensure the initial test was not a fluke). Once the approach is satisfactorily validated, they authorize rolling out a full-blown offensive. Every dollar that can be spent, in an effective way, is allocated to accelerate the accomplishment of their mission. Since we began our partnership with this ministry, we've seen more than 230% growth in their donor base! Even more importantly, the mission of this thought-leading ministry is being accomplished at what feels like the speed of light!

Now, I fully realize how absurd this Rule #67, *Spend as Much as You Need to Raise Money*, might appear, but when God has placed highly inspired leadership into a ministry that is impacting millions, if not billions, of His people, money is not the focal point. It is not the place to conserve. Some ministries are currently comforted by sizeable endowments or have received large bequests. But saving and changing lives is what our faith is all about. Our world is crying out for justice, peace and love. I'm greatly encouraged whenever I see ministry leadership decide to spend down their endowments or allocate estates and bequests to vital ministry priorities.

As a fundraiser, I can tell you that the old "proverb" that *money follows ministry* is absolutely true. I have often seen donors increase their giving to ministries who are totally focused on accomplishing their mission. Sometimes it requires a little more faith to release built up reserves to fund ministry growth. I have also seen how that faith is rewarded through increased giving by their donors.

Isn't it wonderful that the Lord chooses to work through His people (including you and me) to accomplish His purposes?

RULE #68
"Reality is your friend (the value of embracing truth)."

I remember some of my very first meetings with the staff of a much-beloved broadcast ministry. There were five or six of us gathered in their small conference room. Having recently been retained as their fundraising consultant, I wanted to make certain that I could help them to identify reasonable fundraising expectations for their ministry.

As with many organizations I've served, they did not have much in the way of fundraising reports for reference as we began. They were known for OUTSTANDING on-air programming, and the broadcast was quite unique in its approach. But most of their energy until this time had been spent in recording meaningful messages, editing them for the air, and ministering to responders to the program, rather than measuring the effectiveness of their fundraising.

My heart went out to them. They were some of the loveliest and most committed ministry staff that I have ever had the privilege to serve, but...bless their hearts, they had no idea how to effectively measure their fundraising efforts. Our first few meetings went something like this:

Q: Do you have any reports indicating what on-air "offers" like books, audio programs and tchotchkes (aka knickknacks) have been the most appealing to your listeners?

A: "Reports?" They would look at each other and then back to me. "We're not big on reports."

Over the course of time we came to know each other quite well, and they began to anticipate my questions and counsel. When our daylong meetings were over, the director would head to her desk and rifle through the drawers, where she would locate her bottle of aspirin and exceed the recommended dosage, all the while saying, "Oh, I feel another Doug Shaw headache coming on!"

After many years of working together, I walked into the same little conference room where we had held our very first meeting, and sitting on the conference table were a large cut-out of an aspirin bottle and a basket filled with several bottles of aspirin. The team was just sitting there, smiling and pointing to their creation when I entered the room. We all laughed uproariously!

By this time though, we had a much more sophisticated reporting system. Our meetings were much more efficient and effective because we knew our metrics (the critical numbers fundraisers use for analytics). Among the data we had acquired were reports that told us:

1. A summary of all income raised year-to-date by source
2. Results for every on-air offer by type, title and count, including the cost of the product and shipping
3. Results for every direct mail appeal, by segment, for every year we had worked together

4. Active donor counts
5. Lapsed donor counts
6. New donor counts
7. Non-donor counts
8. Reactivation rates for lapsed donors
9. Attrition rates for their donor file
10. Donor acquisition results by source

Together we had built a fundraising program that was highly measureable and accurate. In short, we knew what was real.

Now, the process we went through to arrive at this place wasn't easy or frustration free. But anyone who has spent any time in an effective direct response fundraising world knows that measuring EVERYTHING is critical. We had "source" or "motivation" codes for absolutely "anything that wiggled." These are simply codes imaged onto a direct mail reply device that allow a fundraiser to identify how to attribute a gift. We did this to help us identify *reality,* i.e., what was producing results versus what we *thought* would work or *wanted* to work.

Each time I would recommend a new report, I could see the team tense up; they were all working extremely hard already, and now I was asking them to do even more. When I began to open my mouth to justify this additional work, they would say, almost in unison, "We know, we know, reality is our friend!" Then we would all laugh and they would reach for the aspirin bottle!

NOTES:

RULE #69

"Being a good neighbor brings credibility to your ministry."

For over 20 years I had the privilege of serving as a fundraising consultant to one of our nation's largest rescue missions. It's a great ministry providing over 1,000 homeless women, men and children with safety, food, shelter, clothing and so much more. To my knowledge, it was the ONLY organization in this large city with a place for what is called intact families, i.e., families where both the husband and wife are present with their children. Most organizations tend to provide services only when the father or mother is out of the picture. This ministry is a very caring community of committed people who understand that families come in all configurations.

But this community also cares about their neighbors too. By this I mean they take into consideration those who live and work next door to them. Let's face it; NOBODY wants to intentionally live next door to a rescue mission. There are street people coming and going at all hours of the day and night. It's not uncommon to see old banged-up cars pulling up and dropping off disheveled loved ones in need of assistance and then driving away.

While I was serving this ministry, they were in the midst of building a very large facility for their men's ministry. Some of the neighbors were absolutely appalled that this place for homeless and addicted men was being built right across the street. Some of them even petitioned the city to prevent this facility from being allowed to build in their neighborhood. For a while relationships became very strained as the ministry found it necessary to make its case to the city magistrates for choosing their location.

The city ended up granting building permits, and the mission moved forward with its plans. But the mission leadership took great care in listening to those who were concerned about all the foot traffic their facility would create. This is an issue for just about every rescue mission. There are often street people who want to sleep near the mission so they can be first in line for meals, showers or clothing.

Many people who are not familiar with the work of rescue missions may not realize some of the issues in working with homeless people. There is often a significant population of street people who do NOT want to follow the rules necessary in order to sleep *inside* a mission, like being sober and not carrying weapons, just to name two. There are also those who just want to be on the streets; they don't want to give up being drunk or high even for a night. These people are often called the "chronic homeless." It was the presence of these people that concerned the nearby business people the most, and understandably so.

Wanting to be good neighbors, the mission's leadership decided to modify their architectural plans, building a courtyard for the chronically homeless people, facing away from local businesses and toward a warehouse district. People who decided to sleep near the mission now had a safer place to sleep, and it was out of sight of local retail and restaurant establishments.

I was there the afternoon of the dedication of this multistory men's recovery center. There was so much excitement. It was not only a dedication ceremony but a surprise "naming event" as well. The building was being named for a couple who were longtime supporters of the mission. Their adult children, grandchildren, great grandchildren, friends and other supporters were all in attendance. When the elderly couple arrived at the event and saw their names on this magnificent facility, they held each other and cried tears of joy and gratitude.

The BIG surprise was from the business owner who had challenged the existence of the facility before the city council. Having been invited to attend, she and her family crossed the street with trays full of beautifully arranged hors d'oeuvres. My eyes filled with tears as I watched them circulating through the celebrating crowd, offering them delicious delights!

This family that owned the restaurant had become good neighbors too! The leadership of this ministry had listened to their concerns and accommodated them as best they could. They had been good neighbors. What a heartwarming example of Rule #69, *Being a good neighbor brings credibility to your ministry.*

There are many other ways for ministries to be good neighbors. Here are just a few:

- Participate in and embrace local civic and government opportunities.
- Volunteer your facilities and/or parking lots for community events and/or meetings.

- Maintain an attractive campus.
- Be generous in assisting other nonprofits in your community with services and fundraising expertise you may have and they might need.
- Ensure your organization's culture exhibits a generous spirit to all.
- Pay your bills on time.
- Establish and practice a policy of generous tipping amongst your staff who do business over meals (people notice these things).
- Remember to tip any service providers, e.g., lawn services, snow removal, window washers, etc., during Christmas.
- Be willing to pay a fair price for wages and purchases without invoking the phrase, "but we're a ministry."

The Scriptures are full of examples to help us think through how our organizations can be seen as good neighbors.

RULE #70
"Ignoring the rules can cause you great harm!"

His name was Freckles. He was a beautiful white stallion with several light brown patches of hair on the backs of his ears. From a distance they were imperceptible.

He was pastured in a large field by himself and could be seen running playfully with his tail raised high. He loved visitors and would nuzzle my hands looking for a carrot or a piece of apple. My parents had only one rule for being in the pasture with Freckles: "Don't ever try to ride him!"

Not only was Freckles a skittish stallion, but he had never been broken and therefore could not be ridden...by anyone, including experienced cowhands.

I was 14 years old and living on a 1200-acre ranch managed by my dad. For me, the loneliness of not having any neighbor kids nearby to play with was more than offset by digging for agates in the "draw," a deeply cut valley in the foothills about a 10-minute walk from our farmhouse.

The draw was a former Native American village. What an exciting place for a young man with an overactive imagination! Here I would go looking for arrowheads and imagine myself a young native brave riding my warhorse Freckles. Of course on TV, native warriors used blankets instead of saddles and ropes for bridles. This was in my mind the day I decided to mount Freckles.

His pasture was about a half mile south of the draw, in a field often used to feed cattle in winter. A small stream provided year-round water, and an old, weathered, gray wooden feed bunker stood near the barbed wire gate to make feeding easier in the winter when the snow stood nearly three feet in depth. When we were feeding cattle, we simply backed our pickup through the open gate, closed it, and broke open several bales of hay. Using my dad's calfskin leather gloves, I would break off flakes of each bale and scatter them inside the length of the feeding bunker. The cows would put their noses between wooden slats in the bunker and greedily grab the edges of the flakes of alfalfa hay and munch to their hearts' content.

But today was a beautiful spring day. There were no cows in the field, so Freckles had the entire place to himself. The spring grasses were about six inches high, and Freckles fed himself. His white lips bore a light shade of green from his grazing, and he looked up sharply when I crawled through the barbed wire fence (being too nervous to open the gate for fear he would run out).

When I extended my hand, Freckles immediately trotted my way, hoping for a treat. I angled over toward the feed bunker, hoping to coax Freckles within reach. Slowly I climbed up onto the lip of the bunker, speaking softly to Freckles. He moved closer to my outstretched hand. I reached over to his ears and stood there, scratching the light brown freckles. He was loving it! Carefully I moved along the edge of the bunker, and Freckles dutifully followed, hoping for the treat I might have for him. This put him sideways to me. To my 14-year-old mind, the time and the place were perfect. Slowly scratching down his neck, I patted him on the back, then leaned out to lay my chest onto him. He didn't seem to mind, so I pulled back and held onto the bunker with one hand to steady myself and raised my left leg, placing my boot onto his back.

He snorted and shook his head. But he didn't go anywhere, so I moved my leg slowly over his back and found myself astride him!

I don't have any recollection of Freckles' movements after that. I just know that my mouth was full of dirt as I lay there face down on the ground. My hands and knees were screaming with pain as I tried to lift myself up and look around to locate Freckles. Spitting dirt and feeling my lip for blood, I slowly rolled over onto my back, looking up at the cloudless blue Central Washington State sky.

I was shaking all over and looked down the length of my body to see the new holes in the knees of my jeans. There was a little blood and dirt visible on the skin. Rolling over, I gingerly made my way to my hurting knees. My brain went into full alert mode as I scanned the gravel driveway all the way up to my house. Whew! Apparently no one had witnessed my humiliation and breaking of the one rule.

Still stunned, I made it to my feet. It was then that I realized my hands were both scuffed and bleeding. Wiping them on my jeans, I examined them more closely and flicked the small pieces of gravel out of the heels of my hands.

Then I heard Freckles snort close behind me. For a moment I froze. Then I felt his nose nuzzling the back of my neck. Turning slowly I faced my mount. He stood there like a puppy who had just enjoyed a romp. I couldn't help smiling as I reached up and stroked his long nose. We were still friends.

It wasn't until my mom found my torn jeans in the hamper that I had to fess up to my insubordination. It's funny now, 50 years later, that I thought I could hide my disobedience by simply throwing my jeans into the hamper.

I was grateful that my mom never mentioned my adventure to my dad. He would not have been as understanding of my breaking of the Freckles rule.

Breaking rules in fundraising may not be as harmful to our bodies as my adventure was to mine. It wasn't long after my day with Freckles that I began to have trouble with my lower back. It has plagued me ever since.

There are serious consequences, however, to breaking the rules of fundraising. Humiliation is one of the least harmful. We can recover from feeling badly about a failed fundraising campaign. The greatest harm is the lost opportunity for maximizing income for the ministry we serve.

When we knowingly break the rules of fundraising, we are putting donated dollars at risk. This is money given to our ministry in trust and the belief that we will do our level best to use it wisely to further our mission.

None of us want to fail. But sometimes our imprudent actions lead us to this place of disappointment. And if we make a habit of not following the rules, we can significantly harm the ministry we serve and even our own reputation.

I see this unfortunate occurrence happening all too often in my role as consultant to nonprofit organizations. It usually begins when a person who does not know the rules of fundraising is appointed to the position of fundraiser. This is exactly why I have written down the rules I have discovered over the past 35 years. It is my sincere hope that nonprofit executives will read both, *The Rules of Fundraising* and *More Rules of Fundraising,* and follow them with great care.

It is also heartbreaking when I see an experienced fundraiser, who knows the rules, give in to the pressures of those they work with and for. I was in this position when I served as a Vice President of Resource Development. It's a painful experience to knowingly forego the rules when peer pressure becomes so strong that we talk ourselves into thinking, "It might work," when everything within us says, "This is not solid fundraising thinking."

This is why this Rule #70 exists, *Ignoring the rules can cause you great harm!*

NOTES:

CONCLUSION

As we began our journey, I expressed my desire for you to see the rules of fundraising for what they really are—a helpful set of tools to encourage you, clear the path ahead of you and give you a craftsman's confidence as you use them in raising funds for your philanthropic cause.

I'd like to think of you sitting in your workshop carefully crafting your ideas, with colleagues running in and out making certain the execution of your plans are being carefully shaped by your mind, heart and hand.

Along the way I've spun a few stories hoping to provide substance and practical examples and to illustrate the best practices of fundraising in a memorable fashion. My main, underlying purpose was to provide you with a toolbox to reach into whenever you desire to sharpen your skills, find a new tool when you need one and provide you with the implements that are familiar to your hand.

My goal has been to help you comprehend that there are indeed rules involved in fundraising. Again, these are not my rules. They are bodies of knowledge known to those who have successfully labored in the fields of philanthropy for decades.

Even though we don't get to make them, we can begin to

search for them like the nuggets of gold they are. Their great value comes from the fact that they are rare knowledge. Learn them and you will greatly enhance your skill and your ability to provide the valuable resources that your ministry so dearly needs.

In no way are these rules a comprehensive compilation. But now that you know to look for them, you too can contribute to the great body of knowledge that drives successful fundraising.

It's my ultimate goal, however, to give you the gift of hope that has been so generously shared with me by the many journeymen and master craftsmen of our trade. After all, we all need each other in this great profession of philanthropic encouragement. Because there's an entire world out there, filled with needs that only the Lord can meet, and he is choosing to do some of it through the exercising of your special craft.

Embrace the journey, discover new rules, use them to soar and articulate them to the rest of us who need all the assistance we can gather to make our needy world a place of hope for those who hurt; a place of fulfillment for those who are hungry for everything that's good. May you have peace and joy on your journey, and may God grant you the wisdom to know that you are not alone and help is nearby.

BIBLIOGRAPHY

Corporation Centre. "Non-Profit Corporations." *coporationcentre.ca*. 2017.

Gelb, Michael J. and Sarah Miller Caldicott. *Innovate Like Edison: the Success System of America's Greatest Inventor.* New York: Penguin Group, 2007.

Jimmy John's. (2011). *Old Coot* [Television commercial]. Retrieved from https://www.youtube.com/ watch?v=NauOTeKRGjs

Kinsella, W.P. *Shoeless Jo*. Boston: Houghton Mifflin, 1982.

Koenig, Rebecca. "Killing Sacred Cows." *The Chronicle of Philanthropy*. 29 February 2016.

Reference. "How fast can a bear run?" *reference.com*. 2017

The Princess Bride. Directed by Rob Reiner (20th Century Fox, 1987).

Field of Dreams. Directed by Phil Alden Robinson (Universal Pictures, 1989).

Scudder, Samuel H. "Look at Your Fish," *Every Saturday: A Journal of Choice Reading*. April 4, 1874.

Tareke, Gebru. *The Ethiopian Revolution: War in the Horn of Africa*. New Haven: Yale University Press, 2009. (pg. 20).

de Waal, Alex. *Evil Days: Thirty Years of War and Famine in Ethiopia*. New York: Human Rights Watch, 1991 (pg. 2 & pg. 5)

Internal Revenue Service. "Section 501(c)(3) Organizations." *https://www.irs.gov/publications/p557/ch03.html#d0e3767,* January 2017.

"Truth Is Stranger Than Fiction." *The Wittenburg Door*. Trinity Foundation, 1971.

Wolfe, Tom. *The Bonfire of the Vanities*. New York: Farrar, Straus and Giroux, 1987.

ABOUT THE AUTHOR

Douglas Shaw is married to Kathryn Shaw and has two grown children, Laura and Graham. He is founder of Douglas Shaw & Associates, Inc. (DSA), a leading, international fundraising consulting firm located in Naperville, Illinois. He has been involved in raising funds for Christian nonprofits for the last 36 years, raising hundreds of millions of dollars for more than 300 nonprofit organizations and ministries. His passions are his faith, family, their thriving business, reading history and fly-fishing. He is a graduate of Simpson University, San Francisco, CA, where he earned a Bachelor of Arts in History in 1975, and completed his graduate work at Fuller Seminary in Pasadena, CA, where he earned a Master of Arts in Theology in 1980.

Today, Douglas serves as the Chairman of the Board/CEO. He is a sought-after speaker on fundraising and leadership. His informal, personal style appeals to audiences of all types, and he is invited to return to almost every venue where he speaks. Doug has conducted special events with entertainment and political celebrities such as George and Barbara Bush, James and Susan Baker, Franklin Graham, Lloyd Ogilvie, Pat Boone, Art Linkletter and former Congressman J. C. Watt. He produced endorsement radio and television commercials with former President Ronald Reagan.

Doug's commitment to ethical fundraising has earned him a reputation as a straight shooter and an effective practitioner of the rules of fundraising. He was encouraged by his clients and colleagues in the philanthropic community to write this book.

Made in the USA
Lexington, KY
10 July 2017